Bible studies on

Jacob

Mark Vander Hart

 Reformed Fellowship, Inc.
3363 Hickory Ridge Ct. SW
Grandville, MI 49418

©2007 Reformed Fellowship, Inc.
Printed in the United States of America
All rights reserved

For information:
Reformed Fellowship, Inc.
3363 Hickory Ridge Ct. SW
Grandville, MI 49418
Phone: 616.532.8510
Web: reformedfellowship.net
Email: sales@reformedfellowship.net

Book design by Jeff Steenholdt

ISBN 978-0-9793677-7-9

Contents

It's Twins! *1*
Selling the Future for Food *11*
Issac Blesses God's Covenant Heir *19*
The Beloved Son Must Flee From His Own Brother *29*
The Lord Awakens Jacob to His Covenant Calling *39*
Jacob Marries the Mothers of Israel *47*
The Struggle for Covenant Children *55*
Jacob Aquires Great Wealth *63*
The Lord Directs Jacob to Leave Laban *71*
Jacob Prepares to Meet His Brother Esau *79*
Jacob Wrestles with a "Mysterious Stranger" at Peniel *87*
Jacob and Esau Meet Again as Brothers *95*
Jacob's Sons Dishonor the Covenant Sign *103*
At Bethel God Reaffirms His Covenant (Again!) *111*
The History of the Older Brother, Esau *119*
Israel and Sons Sojourn in Egypt *127*
By Faith Jacob Blessed Joseph's Sons *135*
Jacob Tells His Sons About the Future *143*

Lesson 1

It's Twins

Read Genesis 25:19-26

The account of Isaac: an introduction
The book of Genesis is put together in a very deliberate way to show to the readers, members of the community of the Christian faith, how God's redemption moves along. We travel from the grand story of the creation down to the point where the family of Jacob would journey from Canaan to Egypt to be kept alive by God through the work of Joseph. Throughout the book we read the phrase, "This is the account . . ." or "These are the generations of . . ." (cf. Gen. 2:4; 5:1, etc.). We meet just such another section again in Genesis 25:19, the account of Abraham's son Isaac.

As is true of several of the other accounts that make up the book of Genesis, this section (which covers Genesis 25:19-35:29) does not focus in great detail upon the man Isaac. In fact, Genesis 26 is really the only major chapter that is devoted to God's story in the life of Isaac. For the rest of this portion of Genesis, much more is devoted to Jacob and, to a lesser extent, to Esau. These accounts are focused on "what became of . . . ." Like so much in Biblical history, there is a forward-looking concern. These accounts move us ahead from one point to another point, from one figure to another figure in redemptive-history. Thus the account of Isaac is going to tell us, in the main, what became of Isaac, what happened in his family.

The opening verses (25:19, 20) quickly tie us into material from the past before moving us ahead to the new story.

The Life of Jacob

The great patriarch Abraham, the father of all believers, has two sons: Ishmael and Isaac. Yet it is Isaac who is the son of the promise, the carrier of all the redemptive-covenant promises (Gen. 21:10, 12). Ishmael gets a brief account (25:12–18) to tell us that indeed God fulfilled His promise to make a nation from Ishmael, a nation that would live in hostility with its neighbors (see Gen. 16:11, 12; 21:13). Once Ishmael's account can be nicely rounded off, then the inspired text turns us back to the main storyline.

Several things are noted: Isaac is Abraham's son, a son of his father's very old age, one who is born when his human parents are as "good as dead" (Rom. 4:19). But God is the God who works redemptive miracles to bring His promises into the world. Salvation is through miraculous and amazing grace!

Isaac marries Rebekah (see Gen. 24). Isaac is forty years old, and he loves Rebekah very much (Gen. 24:66). Furthermore, Genesis 25:20 underlines the fact that Rebekah is an Aramean, very closely related to her husband Isaac. The issue of marriage and whom one marries will come back again and again in this story of Jacob. Abraham had not wanted his son to marry any of the Canaanite women, and so he had sent his servant back to the northern area of the Fertile Crescent, to the region of Paddan-Aram, in order to seek a wife from among his relatives. Later on, of course, Jacob will return to this same region. Already now, the reader hears Laban mentioned, Rebekah's brother and Jacob's uncle, the man who will play an important role in the wives and the wealth that Jacob will acquire. One might say that the text is "looking ahead" for us at this point.

Another barren wife (25:21)

Students of the Bible are well aware of the fact that Sarah, Abraham's beautiful wife, was barren and unable to

It's Twins!

have children. Yet God gave the miracle of a baby boy when she was very old! This is amazing, enough to make people smile and laugh (Gen. 21:6). But now we read of another beautiful wife, Rebekah, who is barren. This raises the question of what God is doing. Will every generation of the promised line have a barren wife? Of course, we may remind ourselves of other women unable at first to have children in redemptive-history (Rachel, the wife of Manoah, Hannah, and Elizabeth in Luke 1). The miracle of life stands out more clearly in the lives of these women when we see how God comes at the right time and in the right way to make the barren woman the joyful mother of children (see Ps. 113:9).

Isaac intercedes for his wife by praying to the LORD for a child. As so many psalms recount that the LORD hears the cries of the needy and those in distress, so the LORD hears Isaac's prayers. Isaac and Rebekah had to wait 20 years before she bears her children (see vs. 20, 26). Our God gives more than enough in that Rebekah becomes pregnant with twins! And this was not a "quiet" pregnancy! The two children in her womb jostle each other. The word in the original suggests "smashing" or "crushing." Are the twins engaged in a kind of pre-natal wrestling match? Certainly the readers know that the younger one will wrestle, years later, in the dark of night with a "mysterious stranger" . . . and will prevail.

Some Jewish rabbis later would interpret this jostling not as sibling rivalry, but rather as Esau trying to kill his twin brother Jacob. Thus the rabbis would say that a person could commit sin *before* one was born. This apparently lies behind the disciples' question in John 9 about the man who was blind from his birth (see John 9:2ff.). But that rabbinical interpretation suggests that God was opposed to Esau because he attacked Jacob in the womb, and God loved Jacob. In other words, God was right to reject Esau because Esau had attempted murder. We might well ask the question: how do we know that it was Esau that attacked Jacob? Could it have been Jacob who attacked Esau? After all, when the boys are born, Jacob has grabbed hold of his brother Esau's heel (v. 26). But perhaps we should not even talk of "attack" here, lest our imagination go too far afield. In any case, God richly blesses the loving couple, Isaac and Rebekah, with twins who vigorously interact with each other already in the womb.

Prayer answered by prophecy (25:23, 24)
Rebekah goes to the Lord for answers about her very active pregnancy. "Why is this happening to me?" This has likely been an emotional roller-coaster: barrenness, followed by prayer; then pregnancy involving two fetuses struggling together, followed (again) by prayer. "Why barren?" is followed by "why this battle?" In fact, Rebekah's question literally reads, "If so, why am I . . . ?" It is an incomplete sentence. Perhaps the thought here is, "We've prayed for pregnancy, but have I received more than I expected?"

The LORD's answer is very specific in terms of making a clear distinction between the children and the destiny of their descendants. Although these are now only two boys in the womb, they will become the fathers of two nations. The younger will come to prominence as the older will serve him. The younger will in fact be the stronger and will prevail. In saying this, the LORD is setting aside the normal practice of giving the oldest (or older) son the firstborn privileges. The firstborn son is the sign of the father's "strength," and that son would normally inherit the double portion of his father's possessions. That was his birthright. Additionally, he would have both privileges and responsibilities to carry on the family's standing, its faith and commitments, and its position in the surrounding society. The firstborn had to be aware of his past (where he came from) and the future of the family (where his descendants, by God's grace, should be).

In this particular family, the firstborn had an even greater calling since this was no ordinary ancient Near Eastern household. This was a family created by the covenant of God's grace in Jesus Christ! The twin boys are not the sons of a concubine or slave girl (cf. Ishmael, born of Hagar). Both boys are born of the legal and rightful wife, Rebekah. And the father Isaac is the son of the free woman, Sarah, born miraculously when she was barren and her body was "as good as dead." But the Word of the LORD sets that aside in this case, and we are not told why this is so. God's plan is carried on out of His inscrutable wisdom and good pleasure.

Election revealed in history
Read Romans 9:1–13, especially verses 10–12.
The Apostle Paul makes reference to two important verses from the Old Testament, both dealing with Jacob and Esau. He is in the midst of a line of thought that reveals God's good pleasure in election. Paul first draws attention to Abraham's children, and there it is clear that Isaac is the child of the gracious promise, while Ishmael is the child "by nature." But the argument must be sharpened with Isaac's children: both Esau and Jacob are children born after barrenness is removed following prayer. Both boys have the same father and the same mother (cf. Rom. 9:10), and Rebekah is a free woman, not a handmaiden or slave woman. Yet the truth of election is already heard as Paul recalls Genesis 25:23, "The older will serve the younger." The second verse is from Malachi 1:2, 3: "Jacob I loved, but Esau I hated." Not the child by nature and not the eldest son, who by social custom was entitled to the privileges of the firstborn son.

The Life of Jacob

The point that the inspired Apostle is driving home here is that nothing *we* do can merit God's electing choice. The works of the law cannot earn credit with God for our salvation. But this is truly an abiding comfort for believers. Since the law of God is a constant reminder of just how far we have fallen short of the glory of God, yet salvation is rooted in God's love for us, not our performance of love for God. We love because He first loved us. When Paul writes in Romans 9:11 that God's purpose in election was announced "before the twins were born or had done anything good or bad," the force of that statement is that God's choice is not because of foreseen goodness later on in Jacob's life. If God chooses Jacob because He saw later goodness in Jacob, then human performance and our merit do lie in the foundation of our salvation. But such an idea is thoroughly repugnant to the believing Christian. When all of humanity deserves condemnation, it is to the praise of God's love and grace that He has elected us to salvation in Christ, through Him alone who died to take away our sins and rose again for our justification.

What is in a name? (25:24-26)

The time arrives for the birth, and just as the LORD had revealed, there are twins. Two boys are born to Isaac and Rebekah, but they are not identical twins, given the fact that their descriptions different. The firstborn is ruddy in his complexion and covered with hair (the technical term is *hypertrichosis*, if you want a big word!). Later on David will also be described as ruddy (I Sam. 16:12; 17:42). The firstborn receives the name Esau, but how that name is related to "hairy" is very unsure. The word for ruddy (red), on the other hand, is closely connected with Esau's other name, which is Edom. This draws our attention to the reason why parents pick particular names for their children: is it to honor a particular relative (grandfather or

It's Twins!

grandmother)? Is it because of some trait noticed already at birth? Or, is a name chosen for a child because it is currently popular and sounds "nice?" What are some reasons in Biblical history why particular individuals receive their names (think of Samuel, Isaiah's sons, and our Lord Jesus [Matt. 1:21]).

We cannot be completely sure what Isaac and Rebekah are thinking as they pick the name Esau for the oldest son. But the second son "makes a name for himself" by his actions during his own birth. He emerges from the womb grasping the heel of his older brother. This interesting incident almost suggests that the struggle in the womb during Rebekah's pregnancy is not over, and the second boy is ready to chase his slightly older brother down. Of course, Jacob as a baby would not be conscious of such a conflict as he grabs his brother's heel. The word for "heel" in the Hebrew language lies at the root of the name the younger twin receives, Jacob. Furthermore, just as his older brother will get another name (Edom, "red") later, so the younger will also receive a second name (Israel) later on. But that story is ahead of us.

The name "Jacob" requires some comment. As a personal name, it is known from extra-biblical sources as "Jacob-el," which likely means, "May God be at (my) heel," that is, "May God protect me." Such a name in fact has quite a positive meaning. So Kidner (*Genesis*, p. 130) sees the name as a kind of prayer: "May God be your rearguard." But the name is also given to irony or a second, almost hostile, meaning. To be at someone's heel implies that one is dogging another's footsteps, trying to trip, to trick, or to deceive someone else. It may very well be that the parents intend a positive spin on the name that they give to Jacob. Yet we should note that the ironical sense of Jacob's name will certainly emerge later on in the lives of the two boys.

The Life of Jacob

Protection (from God) as well as deception (by Jacob) will be often seen in Jacob's life. Read Hosea 11:12–12:4. In this covenant indictment of God's people the prophet Hosea draws attention to the sins of the south (Judah) and the north (called Jacob in v. 2). Israel (i.e., Ephraim) is Jacob, full of lies and deception. He has been a struggling nation, even as he emerged from the womb.

Clearly, God's election is not based upon the goodness of Jacob and his descendants, the people of Israel. God's election is rooted in His own loving purposes in Christ. The Bible's teaching about original sin (we are both guilty and polluted from the womb) humbles us, only to make us see the amazing nature of God's grace to save us apart from any merit of our own.

Lesson 1: Points to ponder and discuss

1. In several places we read that God describes Himself as the "God of Abraham, the God of Isaac, and the God of Jacob." Then why does the patriarch Isaac get much less textual attention in the book of Genesis? What role does Isaac play in redemptive-history?
2. Redemptive-history in the Bible has a number of barren women who play a very important part in the story. Why are there (apparently) so many of them in redemptive-history? What point is God making with us?
3. Psalm 113 is noted in the lesson above. Read through this entire psalm. What several things does it say about God? How are these truths about God shown to us in the story of the birth of the twins, Esau and Jacob? How are these same truths revealed to us in the stories of Abraham and Isaac earlier?
4. Isaac prays for his barren wife, and Rebekah goes to seek out an answer from the LORD during her rather

turbulent pregnancy. Prayer plays an important part in the parents' lives here. God answers these petitions with pregnancy and then with prophecy. How does God answer prayers today? Does He ever not answer our prayers? What does the Bible teach us about prayers that appear to us to go unanswered?

5. God reveals the future to Rebekah concerning her sons. Can we believe that she then told this prophecy to her husband Isaac? To her sons Esau and Jacob as they were growing? Why or why not? What difference might it have made whether she told or did not tell the prophecy to her husband and/or her sons?

6. Verse 23 says that "one people will be stronger than the other, and the older will serve the younger." Does this word from the LORD mean that conflict was inevitable between the two nations? Why or why not? From where do conflicts and fighting come?

Lesson 2

Selling the Future for Food

Read Genesis 25:27–34

Introduction
Already at birth it becomes apparent that these twin boys are quite different. The slightly older boy (Esau) emerged from the womb covered with hair (a physical thing that makes him clearly a fraternal twin to his slightly younger brother Jacob). Identical twins they are not! Furthermore, the LORD had revealed that the relationship of these children would not be friendly. As the heads of nations, their future and that of their descendants would not be that of equals. The one nation would be stronger than the older; the "older will serve the younger" (Gen. 25:23).

Separate developments (25:27–28)
These two verses are something of a transition that bridge the story line from the birth and naming parts to the separate developments that occur in these two lives.

Twins often grow up close to each other, even physically close. But this does not appear to happen in the tent of Isaac. Esau develops into a skilled hunter, while Jacob is content to remain around the tents of his semi-nomadic family. Furthermore, we note that there is the reality of parental favoritism: Isaac loves Esau because he hunts, and when successful, that means delicious wild game to eat. Rebekah, on the other hand, loves the younger son Jacob, but the text does not give us a reason why. It may be because of the LORD's word during her pregnancy. But readers know that when parents show favoritism to particular children, the end result is almost always not pleasant.

The Life of Jacob

In the description of what these two sons are like, it is easy for our cultural stereotypes to take over as we read this very familiar story. A common way to read this story is to think that Esau is "all-boy," a regular guy who loves to play football, baseball, and rugby. He is not afraid to go out on the hunt to kill and prepare game. Jacob, on the other hand, is a kind of "momma's boy." While twin brother Esau is outside doing "guy things," Jacob is back with mother Rebekah, baking cookies, perhaps. In other words, Jacob is soft, maybe a kind of sissy. If that is the picture that we see as we read this story, then Jacob comes off quite unfavorably. As he grows up, we already don't "like" Jacob.

But let us consider this story again. Earlier in the story of Genesis, we met a great hunter before the LORD, Nimrod. While there is nothing wrong with hunting for game in order to eat, Nimrod is not noted for his godliness. Furthermore, father Isaac does not admire or show his love to son Esau for his godliness. It is his stomach that is satisfied by the delicious game that Esau is able to bring back from his hunts. Favoritism in family relationships based on self-satisfaction is a minefield of dangers. Trouble brews before trouble breaks out.

As for Jacob being a dweller in tents, there is nothing unusual about that. In fact, that is what semi-nomads do: they live in tents! Thus Jacob is living in a manner not unlike his own father and grandfather before him. In addition, Jacob is described in verse 27 as a "quiet man" (NIV). Other translations say "perfect" or "complete." Currid (*Genesis*, vol. 2, p. 19) says that Jacob was "a man of peace." The word used here is usually translated in a moral sense, i.e., perfect. See Job 1:1 and 8, as well as Genesis 6:9. Both Job and Noah are described as "perfect." This does not mean that they were free from original sin. Rather it refers to the fact that they were godly men who lived before the LORD God with integrity, seeking to serve God in faithfulness.

Selling the Future for Food

Is this the sense that this word has in Genesis 25:27? Hamilton (*Genesis 16–50*, p. 177) thinks that the moral sense as descriptive of Jacob is "inappropriate" here. He interprets the sense here as "complete," meaning that Jacob is "a self-contained, detached personality complete in himself, hence 'quiet.'" Others disagree in order to maintain that Jacob is a morally upright man as he grew up, and that understanding must be used to judge, in the main, his actions in the rest of his life. What does his later life show? Is Jacob "soft?"

Swearing away the birthright (25:29–33)

There are a number of ways of reading what happens in this part of the story. How you read this will influence how you think of the two characters, especially Jacob. It is often read in the following manner: brother Esau comes back from a hunt, but he is so very hungry (apparently he caught and killed nothing for food), that he is truly on the verge of death. He asks for a bowl of red soup from his twin brother, but his brother drives a very hard bargain. Esau is somewhat trapped: either sell the birthright and live (by eating the soup), or, refuse to sell the birthright but then risk his own life since, in his mind, "I am about to die" (v. 32). In this way of reading and hearing the story, Jacob comes across quite unfavorably. Even if Esau is not really about to die from hunger, Jacob should have done the "nice" thing, the Christian thing: he should have given his brother a bowl of hot red soup and a second helping, if he asked! Some writers even say that Jacob here "steals" the birthright away from his very hungry brother.

But there is another way to hear the story if we think our way through the details. First of all, we will learn later in Genesis 27 that Esau also is able to cook. When Isaac sends him away on the hunt, Esau will be successful then, and he will come back, cook his catch, and present it to his father Isaac.

The Life of Jacob

Second, can we really believe that Esau is on the verge of dying of starvation? How long does it take for a person to die of starvation, if he or she is deprived of food (assuming that such a person has water to drink)? Normally starvation takes several weeks. Plus, a person on the verge of death from starvation is so weak that they cannot move without assistance. In addition, such a person does not take red stew (lentil soup?) for his first meal on the road to recovery. It would be too great a shock to the starving person's system. Fruit juices usually start the starving back to health.

Okay, let's say that Esau was very hungry. Indeed, when have we not heard our children say—or said it ourselves—"I'm starving! When are we going to eat?" It is very believable to think that Esau has not had much if anything to eat while he was away on the hunt. But when he says that he is about to die, we find that to be very hard to believe. Esau is exaggerating his growling stomach.

But to the more difficult question, we ask this, "Was Jacob being an oppressor, a cheat, when he drove this bargain with his brother?" Commentator Baldwin (*Genesis 12–50*, p. 106) thinks so. "Jacob was ruthless in his scheming to outwit his brother, who, as the elder of the two, was in a specially privileged position." Again, we must ask ourselves whether this is true. How is Esau outwitted? Jacob's proposition is fairly straightforward: "I'll give you some of this red stuff, and you give me the birthright." That is the deal: take it or leave it. No small print; no unseen or unspoken clauses, amendments, or modifications.

What was the birthright, in any case? Why would Jacob want it? We know from later in the story of Genesis 27 that the birthright and the blessing are separate things.

The birthright was the privilege that belonged to the firstborn son. This was the favored gift that the firstborn son was to receive, namely, that he would receive the double portion from his father. Read Deuteronomy 21:15–17,

Selling the Future for Food

where the law requires that the firstborn son receive just such a portion, even if he is not the son of the beloved wife. Such a double portion would put the son in a favored spot for the future, and he naturally would be the leading figure in the family's future, all things being equal. This was in Esau's future prospects, and it is this birthright that Jacob wishes to acquire. Why? Here we might speculate. Perhaps Jacob is a selfish man, a person who sees his twin brother at a slight disadvantage and then he goes in "for the kill." But, on the other hand, if he is a "perfect" man in a moral sense, it is more likely that he sees in his brother a lifestyle, a spiritual direction, and a moral personality that cares little for the things of God's covenant. Jacob and Esau are the sons of the same two parents, but they are headed in different directions spiritually and covenantally, at least at this point in the story. If Esau really values the birthright for all the right reasons (or, for that matter, for any reason at all!), then he would refuse to sell the birthright. But the smell of the red stew is enticing, and it is ready to eat now, and what good is a birthright (a future thing) now when one is about to die (present predicament)? He sells the birthright, even sealing the deal by swearing an oath at Jacob's insistence (v. 33).

Jacob serves his brother a very delicious meal (hunger makes for a good appetite, after all!) of bread and soup. The original text in verse 34 is rather blunt in the use of four words (all verbs): "(he) ate . . . drank . . . got up . . . left." Some commentators say that in the ancient Near East the hairy person is considered to be boorish and crude. In this case, Esau seems to live up to the stereotype! But there is one more verb in verse 34: (he) despised. Esau has just sold his birthright, confirming the sale with a solemn oath or vow, and the Bible tells us that this means he despised his birthright.

The Life of Jacob

Esau despised his birthright (25:34)

Despise. Sounds so harsh, does it not? Does Esau ever say anything mean and nasty about the birthright? It does not seem so. The word "despise" has the idea of thinking little of something, treating something with little or no honor. What we love and value, we protect and hold onto. We would not let something go, but we would think about it often, and we would consider it very valuable. But to despise something is like wiping our dirty shoes on a doormat. We probably don't hate the doormat, but we don't highly value it either. When David sinned with Bathsheba, God tells David that he has despised the Word of the LORD (II Sam 12:9). Esau faces a far-reaching choice: a bowl of soup versus the birthright? Esau here thinks with his stomach.

What has he just done? Does he have any idea what it means to sell his birthright as a covenant son for a bowl of red stew? Genesis 25:34 closes this account with the somber statement: "So Esau despised his birthright." What Esau has done is to seek a short-term solution to a growling stomach and physical weakness due to his great hunger. But this indifference and apathy to his great privilege as the firstborn son is equivalent to hostility. It is interesting to note that we do have ancient texts that tell us that it was possible for a person to sell his birthright. Yet we may not evaluate Esau's actions here merely in the light of ancient traditions and customs. The text of Scripture says that Esau's actions were in reality a despising of his birthright.

Jacob, on the other hand, has looked ahead to obtain the blessing that accompanies the covenant promises. Jacob is often treated harshly for what he did, but this should be re-examined. Did Jacob sense in his brother that the things of God and of His covenant were not important to Esau? Did Jacob think that perhaps rather than have the covenant responsibility fall to a man who was largely indifferent to

Selling the Future for Food

the coming of the Kingdom of God, he would "step up to the plate" and try to secure this birthright with all its privileges but also its responsibilities as well? If that is the case, who then is the wiser man? When the story began, Jacob had lentil soup, while Esau had the birthright. When the narrative closes, it is reversed: Jacob has the birthright, while Esau is satisfied with a nice square meal. Hours later Esau will be a hungry man again. Who is now the richer man?

Read Hebrews 12:16–17. In the context of this passage (Heb. 12:14–17) the inspired text is urging us readers to live in peace and in holiness, to avoid allowing little sinful weeds to pop up, such as bitterness and sexual immorality. In that context he refers to Esau who is described as godless or profane because he sold his inheritance rights as the eldest for a single meal (12:16). Paul rightly describes such people as enemies of the cross of Christ, people whose god is their stomach, folks who mind earthly things (Phil. 3:18, 19). Are such people with us today? Is such a warning for us as well?

Esau and Jacob were both covenant sons. They both were called to seek God's rule over all things in their life. Spiritual wisdom opened Jacob's eyes to the future, the long-term future, in fact. But Esau sold his future for some tasty food, and thus he lost it all.

Lesson 2: Points to ponder and discuss

1. Why does Rebekah love Jacob? Are there some hints or suggestions in the story that may explain why she loves him more than Esau?
2. Genesis 3:15 tells us that there is a history-long battle and struggle going on between the Seed of the woman and the seed of the serpent. How is such a struggle

The Life of Jacob

evident in the story of these two brothers as they grow up in the family of Isaac and Rebekah?
3. Christians are under no obligation to assist the wicked in their agenda and program of working against the Kingdom of God. Yet Christians are required to feed our enemies when they are hungry and give them drink when they are thirsty. Read Romans 12:20. How can we sort this out? Talk about those times when you have (or could have) shown Christian charity to those who were your enemies.
4. We are baptized into the Name of the Triune God. That is our Christian birthright in the covenant of grace. What do we have as Christians in such a birthright? What privileges and responsibilities now fall to us with the name "Christian"?
5. What parallels are there, if any, between the first temptation in the Garden of Eden (food that could make one wise), what the first woman and first man did, and this action of Esau? Both stories deal with food as a kind of temptation. What did our first parents lose, and what did Esau lose?
6. The third commandment deals with misusing God's Name. How can Christians themselves sometimes despise God's Name, besides cursing and blaspheming? Can we treat God's Name lightly? How does heresy (false teaching, unbiblical doctrine) belong to the area of despising God's Name?
7. Esau had a "felt need," namely hunger. We all have real and pressing needs, including physical needs. What does our Lord Jesus Christ press upon us about His Kingdom and our "needs" in Matthew 6:25–34?

Lesson 3

Issac Blesses God's Covenant Heir

Read Genesis 27:1–29

Introduction

We were introduced to the twins Esau and Jacob in Genesis 25. The story told there shows that the two boys are in conflict. But the conflict has not yet broken out into the open. Prophetic word (Gen. 25:23) has assigned Jacob over Esau the firstborn. Jacob purchases the birthright from Esau, and Scripture tells us that Esau has despised his birthright (Gen. 25:34).

Genesis 26 is something of a "detour" in the story of Jacob, such that Isaac comes across as a kind of valley or lower plateau between the "taller mountain peaks" of Abraham and Jacob. Yet even in that chapter we may read with gratitude to God that He keeps His covenant words to the godly patriarchs. Isaac clearly hears an echo of Genesis 12:1–3 as he too is promised God's presence, His blessing, the land, and many descendants, through whom blessing will go to other nations (see Gen. 26:2–5).

Genesis 26:34–35 brings Esau back into the story, and the topic here is his marriage to two Hittite women. It is interesting to note that he will marry a third wife, Mahalath (an Ishmaelite), in Genesis 28:8–9. In this way, brief notices about his wives serve as a kind of "bookend" that surrounds the story of Jacob receiving the blessing from his father Isaac in Genesis 27.

The Life of Jacob

"I think I'm going to die soon" (27:1-4)

Genesis 27 has been called "a chapter saturated with intrigue, suspense, and agony" (J. J. Davis, *Paradise to Prison*, p. 236). The subjects of food and death, death and food, are fascinating ones, subjects that come together in these stories. Esau had come back from hunting, exhausted, and he talks as if he is going to die. So he sells his birthright to get some good soup (Gen. 25:29ff.).

Isaac now is old, and he senses that death cannot be too far away. But he would love to eat Esau's food before he pronounces his blessing. Both men exaggerate the prospects of their deaths. Esau eats the stew and walks away. And Isaac does not die until Genesis 35:29! "Reports of their deaths have been greatly exaggerated!"

In any case, Isaac tells his son Esau to hunt for some wild game. With success in the hunt, Esau can cook up some really tasty food. This will be the occasion for patriarch Isaac to give his blessing to the firstborn son, a kind of reading of his "last will and testament" before he dies. It may very well be that the game caught in the hunt would provide the food for a kind of private feast that would enhance the blessing presentation.

But there is something wrong in all this. The granting of a blessing was not a secret affair between a father and his son. If anything, it was a public event, a cause for community acknowledgment and celebration. What is more, would it not be expected that Isaac should include the whole family—his wife Rebekah and his other son Jacob—in this granting of the blessing? Is the momentous occasion of pronouncing a blessing a private matter?

Furthermore, the normal practice of giving a double portion to the oldest son means that there is some blessing left for the remaining son(s). But what portion does Isaac give to the son in front of him? Read verses 27-29 and 38-40. It sounds as if Isaac gave virtually the entire blessing

Issac Blesses God's Covenant Heir

away, with little left for the other son. In other words, Isaac was not intending to give a double portion to Esau with another portion to Jacob (let's say, two-thirds for Esau, with one-third to Jacob, so that Esau gets "double"). It appears that Isaac planned to give Esau the near entirety of blessing to Esau; Jacob perhaps could get the scraps.

Whose god is their belly
On one level, we are not completely surprised by this. In Genesis 25:28 we read that Isaac loved the taste of the wild game that Esau hunted. By now his twin sons are in their late 70s (perhaps 77 years of age, when figured according to all the verses that give us ages). Yet Isaac is still motivated by his taste buds and stomach. Has Isaac learned nothing? But much more significant: can he not bring his actions in line with God's revealed Word? It is very difficult to believe that Rebekah had not told Isaac what God had said in Genesis 25:23, perhaps almost immediately after the LORD had revealed the future. "The older will serve the younger." It is quite likely that the text would have read, "Rebekah kept the matter in her heart," or something similar, if she in fact had kept the prophecy all to herself. Thus it is reasonable to believe that Isaac knew that God's covenantal election rested with Jacob, not Esau. But Isaac's love for Esau and his tasty venison outweighs what God has said. Is this one reason why Rebekah is not invited to the blessing ceremony? Does Isaac think that his wife would have protested vigorously the proceedings?

Another factor to be taken into account has already been mentioned in Genesis 26:34–35. Esau had married Hittite wives, and "they were a source of grief to Isaac and Rebekah." Isaac is not happy with his daughters-in-law! When Esau marries at age 40, he has shown no godly wisdom in the choice of his wives. Does this reality not say

The Life of Jacob

anything to father Isaac as to what really lives in the heart of his son Esau? Will Isaac, in effect, continue to enable Esau to prosper in this direction of covenant rebellion by giving him the blessing?

It could be argued that Isaac's decision to bless Esau puts Isaac at enmity with God. God's will is that younger Jacob have dominion over the older Esau. Through this arrangement the Christ would come to save all God's people. Isaac's fatherly choice is not God's choice in election. In this way, Isaac's plan for a private party to give the blessing to Esau is an action that is opposed to the Christ. This does not mean that Isaac has become an unbeliever or that he would not be saved by God's grace. We think here of Peter boldly saying that Jesus is the Christ, the Son of the living God (Matt. 16:16). But a few verses later he is rebuked ("Get behind me, Satan!") when he speaks against what Christ says would happen to Him in Jerusalem (Matt. 16:21-23). How easily we can blind ourselves to God's will in certain areas of life. Isaac, like Esau before him, is here thinking with his stomach and acting out of his fondness toward his firstborn. Isaac loves the son whom God does not love in His covenant. Isaac thus plans to strengthen God's "enemy" at the expense of God's chosen son, Jacob.

Rebekah's reaction (27:5-17)

Ancient Near Eastern tents did not have sound-proof curtain walls, and it is easy to imagine the conversation between Isaac and Esau being overheard. Rebekah (and you the readers, of course!) knows what is going on, and she now moves into action. She does not have a confrontation with her husband about this plan to bless Esau in private. Would a discussion (or even an argument) at this point have made Isaac change his mind?

Issac Blesses God's Covenant Heir

Rebekah takes charge. She tells Jacob what to do, saying, "Listen to my voice" (or, "Do what I say"; see vs. 8, 13, 43). Jacob should kill two choice goats so that Rebekah can cook up some delicious meal for Isaac. The goal in this plot is *to get Isaac's blessing* before his death (v. 10). Jacob's response in verses 11–12 is interesting. He does not question the morality of this plan, but rather its feasibility. "Can we get away with this?" Physically, the boys are different: Esau is hairy, while Jacob is smooth-skinned). Their voices differ (v. 22). If Isaac uncovers this trick, he will curse Jacob, and then all will be lost.

But Rebekah is resourceful: Esau has some clothes still in his parents' tent, they fit Jacob suitably, and some hairy goatskins on the exposed parts of Jacob's body will give Isaac the impression that he is touching Esau. Without further question, Jacob gets the goats, and Rebekah cooks up a great meal.

Whom can you trust?

It was one thing for Jacob to buy the birthright from Esau. Ancient practices allowed that possibility. But the blessing was another matter. Only Isaac could give it, and it was not for sale. Jacob must acquire it by deception. To use a modern idiom: Jacob was a "smoothie." And we wonder what Esau is thinking: having sold his birthright earlier to Jacob, does he think that he still retains the right to receive the covenantal blessing? Doesn't Esau realize that the earlier sale means he has now forfeited his right to this blessing?

Without doubt Rebekah and Jacob engage in deception here against Isaac. Commentators have generally condemned Rebekah and Jacob for this deception of Isaac, and the language used to condemn the mother and her son range from strong denunciation, as if it were the greatest evil, to language that rebukes them somewhat more mildly. Calvin also says that their actions were not right, describing this as a lie, "not a legitimate method of acting." But he

The Life of Jacob

also says that they acted from a strong faith. "Both believe," says Calvin. Rebekah's faith was "mixed with an unjust and immoderate zeal," he writes. In other words, she had a proper goal in mind, but her means were not right. After all, does God need human help to achieve His purposes? Do believers have to take matters into their own hands to "help God along?"

At the same time, we might consider this as well: Rebekah knew God's selection of Jacob. Esau had forfeited all claim to the blessing. Isaac was acting improperly in this regard. To argue with Isaac would be fruitless, at this point. Time is wasting, and so she, as a mother with some authority, comes up with this clever strategy. She is working here not against a man whose actions where holy and blameless, but a man who is acting against God's revealed Word. In any case, what a sad situation now unfolds before us!

Questions and answers (27:18–26)

The story now becomes something of a nail-biter, as Jacob brings the food before his blind father. Yet Isaac is not unobservant, although his eyes do not recognize who is before him. "You're back awfully soon, my son." Jacob uses the LORD's Name to say that God gave him game quickly. "You sound like Jacob, but you feel like Esau." Isaac wants to be sure. "Are you really my son Esau?" he asks in verse 24. Why is he so concerned about it being the son he intends to bless? Because once he pronounces the blessing (verbal oaths were legally binding), then the deed is done. Once Isaac has blessed, the "ink is dry," and there is no recall of his words. So Isaac needs proof of identity, for he is determined to bless Esau, but he must be sure it is Esau. On that point, he has no second thoughts.

"By faith Isaac blessed . . ." (27:27–29)

The occasion is momentous, and father Isaac seeks a kiss

Issac Blesses God's Covenant Heir

from his son. Jacob is misleading a blind man (his father), and he seals the deal with a kiss. Although he has little or no sight, Isaac relies on his other senses: hearing, touching, tasting, and smelling. His doubts are set aside as he proceeds to pronounce the blessing.

The blessing contains important features, and we do well to consider them:

1. "... the smell of a field that the LORD has blessed." These opening words remind us that the blessings we experience around us are from the Creator God and from Him alone.

2. "May God give you of heaven's dew ... grain and new wine."

Here are blessings that come from creation itself. Dew is singled out in Isaac's statement. Dew, especially heavy dew, is very important in parts of the world that have dry, rainless seasons. As the temperature plummets at night, moisture can form on plants and soil to provide just enough sustenance for vegetation that might otherwise dry out and die. See Deuteronomy 33:13 (blessing for Joseph). This is why Elijah's prayers held back both dew and rain during the time of Ahab's apostasy (I Kings 17:1). God even compares Himself to dew in Hosea 14:5a (cf. Zech. 8:12; Prov. 19:12; Job 29:19). Isaac also speaks of abundant grain and new wine. Food and drink are needed to sustain a people; famine was a curse from God.

3. "May nations serve you ... bow down to you."

This part of the blessing takes us to the realm of social relationships, specifically the dominion that God's people will be given. This blessing, in fact, recalls what the LORD had said to Rebekah in Genesis 25:23, "One people will be stronger than the other." It recalls those words but only in part. Isaac believes that he is blessing Esau in such a way that Jacob and all his descendants will serve Esau. As such, as far as his intentions are concerned, Isaac is speaking in direct contradiction to God's Word. Yet his words are being

The Life of Jacob

spoken to God's chosen covenant son Jacob.

We cannot neglect noting that these words will ultimately be fulfilled in a later chosen covenant Son, the Lord Jesus Christ. He will experience shame and a hellish death, but then He will be highly exalted, given a Name above every name. He will be given all authority in heaven and on earth, and through the preaching of the gospel, He will draw all people to Himself. At the Name of Jesus Christ, every knee shall bow in all created reality (see Phil. 2:5–11).

4. "May those who curse you be cursed and those who bless you be blessed."

These words repeat the similar covenant promises spoken many years before to father Abram in Genesis 12:3. So we note God's faithfulness from generation to generation. The content of His promises are not diminished over time, but rather He underscores them as valid when Isaac blesses his son. Hebrews 11:20 says, "By faith Isaac blessed Jacob and Esau in regard to their future." Although Isaac has unrighteously favored Esau, at least it can be said that Isaac believed God's promise was true and that its content was substantial. Everyone who curses the favored son will experience God's curse, but blessing will come to anyone who blesses that son.

We also must not fail to observe that Isaac ascribes all blessing as coming from God (see v. 28, literally, "the God"): "May God give you . . ." There are no blessings apart from the true LORD of heaven and earth. "This is my Father's world," and from His Fatherly hand alone come the blessings that truly enrich the gifts of His creation. From our Almighty God we receive all the vast benefits of creation and re-creation.

Issac Blesses God's Covenant Heir

Lesson 3: Points to ponder and discuss
1. Isaac is blind; he has great difficulty seeing physical things around him. How is he "blind" in other ways in this story? How do Christians have "blind spots" in their own lives?
2. Isaac says he does not know the day of his death (27:2). None of us really do. What does the Scripture say about our life spans (see Ps. 49 and Ps. 90:9–12, for example)? Why do younger people typically think and live as if they are invincible? Is it morbid to think about your own death? How should we think about it?
3. Paul says some people make their belly (appetite) a god (see Phil. 3:19). Various kinds of pleasures can be addicting to some people, although not to others. Some things become idols, false gods. How can we spot such idols in our own hearts and lives? How can such idols be broken and our lives be delivered?
4. Read Colossians 3:9–10; Heidelberg Catechism, Lord's Day 43 (Q/A 112); Westminster Larger Catechism, Q/A 143–145; and Shorter Catechism, Q/A 76–78. The 9th commandment forbids bearing false witness against our neighbor. Yet there are instances in the Bible of people who engage in deception against God's enemies (e.g., the Hebrew midwives in Egypt, Rahab in Jericho, and Jael in Judges 4). Are there times when deception may be legitimate (e.g., spying in time of war, battle strategies)? How do we resist "situational ethics" in this area?
5. Where is God in all these events of this story? What is His particular purpose in these events? Read Romans 8:28. What perspective can this verse (or other verses) give to what has happened here?

Lesson 4

The Beloved Son Must Flee From His Own Brother

Read Genesis 27:30–28:9

Introduction

In the first part of Genesis 27 we read of events in a covenant home where no one seems to trust the other members, where parental favoritism sets into motion some very ungodly actions, and where we are embarrassed to think of these people as our spiritual ancestors. Again, we must wonder: why does God even bother with such? Yet He does, because He is rich in mercy. When Isaac had planned to give the covenantal blessing to Esau, his favorite son, Rebekah then counters this with a plan of deception in which Jacob brings the goat-meat dish to his father. Once a suspicious father Isaac has the reasonable assurance that it is Esau who is before him, he pronounces the rich blessing upon his son . . . Jacob! Isaac believed that this blessing would truly bear its intended fruit as God would fulfill His own word through the blessing.

Deception revealed (27:30–33)

Rebekah and Jacob had to work quickly to prepare their meal of goat meat and to camouflage Jacob with Esau's clothes and goat skins. What if God had given Esau quick success in the hunt (as Jacob would claim for himself; v. 20)? Indeed, Jacob has barely left his father's presence when Esau returns from his own hunt. The story reads almost like a soap opera and a cliff-hanger at that. We can only imagine what a scene that would have erupted if Esau had come

The Life of Jacob

back even earlier and entered father Isaac's tent, only to discover twin brother Jacob dressed in disguise! Esau cooks up a delicious venison dinner (does goat taste like venison, if probably cooked with spices?). He invites his father to the dinner table, so to speak, as he enters the tent. But now comes a tremendous shock to father Isaac as the deception becomes known. Verse 33 says that he trembled violently. It hits Isaac with great force as this reality dawns upon him: he, as covenant head and father, has given the blessing, so full and rich, to someone not his favorite firstborn son, Esau. The deed is done; the word has been spoken, and that oral contact was now legally binding. No turning back now! Isaac tells the equally surprised Esau, "I blessed him—and indeed he will be blessed."

It may very well be the case that Isaac (and Esau as well) are stunned back into reality, God's reality, at this point. If we may safely assume that Isaac had become aware of the LORD's prophetic word in Genesis 25:23—although to this point he has acted contrary to it—yet now he must face this stark reality: Jacob, the younger son, has received the great covenant blessing. There is nothing that Isaac can do about it, for in those days one could not say on such an occasion, "Oops! I made a mistake." Isaac's words are valid, as today we would say, "That is his signature; it is his handwriting." Isaac believed that the promised blessing of God would go to the son he blessed. Only, Isaac meant it for Esau, but God's will is done here: Jacob will receive the blessing. The truth of Proverbs 19:21 is seen in this story: "Many are the plans in a man's heart, but it is the LORD's purpose that prevails." Both Isaac and Esau have now been stunned into seeing God's reality, His truth. But can they handle the truth? How will they handle this truth?

The Beloved Son Must Flee From His Own Brother

"Though he sought the blessing with tears" (27:34)
If Isaac is stunned by these events, so is Esau. This 77-year-old man now bursts into tears. He had wanted this blessing as a lasting confirmation of his father's love but also as a means to prosper in the future. Esau too was going along with his father's ungodly scheme, but the news that their plan had ended in ruin brings about this pathetic scene as the enormity of his loss becomes clear to him. Esau sobs because he realizes his dreams for a prosperous future via the blessing were gone.

Read Hebrews 12:16–17. The Word of God warns us to reject immorality and godlessness. Esau is a prime example of godlessness, such covenantal carelessness. He sold his birthright, despising it, rejecting his high calling, privilege, but also his important responsibility. Yet he wanted the material prosperity. In other words, he wanted all the benefits of God's Kingdom but none of the serious effort. Does this sound familiar in our day as well? Esau had forfeited his claims to the blessing, but he retained a strong sense of entitlement. "Bless me—me too, my father!" he cries.

God's covenantal rule of His world does not operate this way. All Esau's sighs and tears will not change this situation. These are not the tears of repentance, a sorrow that leads to godliness. These are the bitter tears of sad disappointment that sweep through the soul of one who has just lost a great fortune.

Esau is left with leftovers (27:35–40)
Isaac sees Jacob's actions as deceitful (v. 35), and Esau readily agrees. In fact, Esau sees in the meaning of Jacob's own name ("heel") the innuendo of deception. The brother who had grabbed the heel at birth has obtained both the birthright and the blessing. Esau calls his loss of the birthright earlier a deception, but we argued in lesson 2 that there was no deception then. For a bowl of soup, Esau sold

The Life of Jacob

his birthright, a foolish deal indeed. Jacob did not deceive him then. But this latest stunt was deception, not of Esau first of all, but of father Isaac.

We should not forget that Esau could enjoy God's blessing if he now submitted to God's will as that became apparent in this episode. Jacob has the great patriarchal blessing. If Esau had submitted to Jacob, thanked the LORD for His guiding hand, and lived in obedience to God's will from now on, he could have enjoyed the LORD's goodness in the ascendancy of Jacob. Throughout the Old Testament we see again and again that when people keep themselves joined to God's chosen man or His people, they may share in those blessings. Recall that Lot prospered when he and his herdsmen were close to Abram, but when they separated in Genesis 13, Lot made his way toward the wicked city of Sodom.

Esau begs for whatever blessing his father may have left to give. In his blessing to Esau (vs. 39, 40), Isaac uses many phrases from his earlier blessing to Jacob, but now they have a slightly different nuance. The land of Edom would not be as fertile as Canaan would be. The Edomites would be forced to submit to the Israelites, but they would fight back, often revolting against Israel and living in enmity with the Israelites. This "blessing" indicates that the Edomites, Esau's children, would not be a weak nation, but in the end they would always be a restless nation.

Beware the root of bitterness (27:41)

It appears that neither Isaac nor Esau find out that Rebekah was the instigator of Jacob's actions. Isaac does not confront his wife or denounce her, but neither does he blame his younger son or denounce him in anger. In fact, it seems that Isaac submits to the situation, and by Genesis 28 he appears ready to move on. Esau as well does not ask his mother why she did such a thing. Both the reader and Jacob know it, but it may very well be that Isaac and Esau do not

The Beloved Son Must Flee From His Own Brother

know that the deception was Rebekah's idea. Instead, Esau holds a grudge against Jacob. But he does not need to act with haste. He can bide his time. He is prepared to wait until his father is dead (which will not occur for 43 more years!). At least Esau wants to spare his father the emotional devastation that would surely follow when brother kills brother. Isaac has shown favoritism to Esau, and Esau is prepared to repay such love by waiting. Ironic, isn't it: even a cold-blooded murderer can have a streak of kindness, provided it is for a mutual friend or ally.

Bitterness and disappointment can grow roots that sink into the soul. Weeds are easy to uproot when they first appear, but if weeds are neglected and are allowed to grow, the roots sink deeper into the soil, and weeds become more difficult to uproot. The same is true with the roots of bitterness.

Esau hates Jacob. Notice in verse 41 that Esau does not identify Jacob as "my enemy" (which he is in his wicked heart), but he calls him "my brother." We clearly hear an echo of the Cain and Abel story (and even an echo of Ishmael and Isaac's conflict in Gen. 21:9). In Genesis 4 we read that two brothers are divided by God's righteous favor as well as unrighteous jealousy and hatred against the other. Cain killed righteous Abel in cold blood. Esau prepares to do the same to Jacob, the man whom God loves in His covenant. God loves Jacob, not on the basis of Jacob's actions, but on God's own sovereign choice, His own mercy.

"Life really is all about *me*," is a confession and religious worldview that lives in the hearts of many people, even people who sit in Christian church pews week after week. That attitude of the soul will inevitably lead to disappointment, frustration, and then hatred, especially when events do not go our way, or someone else has something that is just a little better, a little nicer, than what we have. Hatred need not express itself as emotional raging and loud outbursts all the time. Hatred can show itself in a

The Life of Jacob

very cool, low-key way that looks for the opportunity to insult, harm or belittle someone. Or, maybe even kill him. Think of how hypocritical Pharisees plotted to attack and destroy our Lord Jesus Christ at an opportune moment. Guard your hearts lest any root of bitterness appear in your soul (cf. Eph. 4:22, 31).

Mother knows best (27:42–26)

Rebekah is informed of Esau's murderous plot, perhaps by a servant, although we cannot be sure. She moves into action. Her actions here show her again taking the initiative to seek protection for her beloved son Jacob. Earlier Rebekah sprang into activity to enable Jacob to obtain the covenantal blessing, and now again she must strategize in such a way to protect Jacob from her older son Esau, who is seething with hatred. Her words in verse 42 suggest that Esau will not be content ("consoled") until Jacob is dead. Does Esau think the blessing will then automatically fall to him if Jacob is dead? Does he imagine that he is the "first runner-up" in some kind of covenant blessing contest? Or, does Esau harbor the idea that, "if I can't have it, then nobody may have it"?

In any case, Rebekah takes charge, and again she tells Jacob to do what she says (verse 43; cf. vs. 8, 13). Jacob must flee to her brother, Uncle Laban, in the Haran region, at the northern part of the Fertile Crescent. Her aim is to allow Esau a "cooling off" period. In her mind, time will heal Esau's hurt feelings, he'll forget the whole episode, and then he will be willing to move on. You know: "forgive and forget." After all, "out of sight" (Jacob gone) will lead to "out of mind" (Esau changing his thinking). If only conflict resolution were that easy.

Rebekah is afraid of losing two of the men in her life (v. 45). It is likely she means that soon after Isaac dies, then Esau will carry out his murderous plot and kill Jacob.

The Beloved Son Must Flee From His Own Brother

Another understanding is that if Esau were to kill Jacob, then the "avenger of blood" would have to execute Esau. Either view seems possible, although I favor the first interpretation.

Rebekah tells a "white lie" to her husband Isaac. She brings up the matter of Esau's Hittite wives to him. On the surface, her complaint is believable. Genesis 26:35 already told us about the irritation that Esau's Hittite wives brought to the parents. Yet Rebekah only mentions her own disgust, allowing Isaac to draw the proper conclusion and to give the appropriate directions. Rebekah had said nothing to Jacob about going away to get a wife, but that will be the operative story for anyone who asks why Jacob has left. The presenting story will be, "Jacob is gone to get the proper wife," but the real story is, "Jacob is fleeing for his life."

Rebekah has used her wiles to advance Jacob so that he will get both: his life and his wife (actually two wives!). But she will never see Jacob again. Too much time will elapse before an "all-clear signal" can be given, but by then Rebekah will have passed away. That signal in fact will never come.

Jacob sent away with blessing (28:1–9)

When we read these verses, we are struck with the impression that Isaac has come around to accept God's will in this matter. Jacob is God's beloved choice. We do not hear any tone of anger or recrimination. True, the issue of getting an acceptable wife is not the real reason that Jacob must leave. Yet he takes his leave with rich words of blessing (again!). Read how many times in verses 1–5 the idea of blessing appears. Jacob receives an even richer expression of blessing here, words embodying the great content of fruitfulness in terms of descendants and possession of the land, "the land God gave to Abraham."

The Life of Jacob

See similar promises in Genesis 15, 17, and 22. Isaac has come around to God's will.

Esau, on the other hand, thinks that if Jacob is out to get a wife that will please his aged parents, he will take a third wife, one from Ishmael's family. Has he learned nothing yet? Esau just does not seem "to get it." He remains spiritually stunted at this point.

Thus this story ends here on a mixed note. Jacob has the blessing, but he also has a brother who hates him, whose anger stews in his heart, as Esau waits for the moment to kill him. Jacob leaves for his family in Paddan-Aram. He has God's blessing, and thus he is a rich man indeed. But he is fleeing his own brother.

Lesson 4: Points to ponder and discuss
1. Some modern commentators have used the word "dysfunctional" to describe Isaac's family. What is meant by that kind of language? And would you agree that this accurately depicts Isaac's family? What is the source of this family's internal struggles and troubles? How does each character contribute, either willingly or unknowingly, to the problems this family experiences?
2. In the Lord's Prayer we pray, "Thy will be done." What was God's will for Esau and Jacob with regard to the blessing? How do we understand this prayerful petition today? Does God's will in this prayer refer to His secret (decretive) will, or to His revealed will? See Deuteronomy 29:29; Heidelberg Catechism, Lord's Day 49 (Q/A 123); WLC, Q/A 192; WSC, Q/A 103.
3. Is Esau's response to Jacob's actions understandable? Is this reaction justifiable?

The Beloved Son Must Flee From His Own Brother

4. God's word in Ephesians 4:22, 31, is that we take care not to allow the root of bitterness to develop among us. But he is addressing the church, God's holy temple, the body of Christ. Do these admonitions from the Apostle Paul even need to be said to Christians? How can disappointment lead to frustration, and even to bitterness? What does God's Word say about how to deal with this?
5. Esau is angry with his brother Jacob, but he controls its expression—for the time being. How do you handle angry people? What does the Bible say should be our response if we know that somebody has something against us?
6. Hebrews 2:1–3 warns against ignoring a great salvation. Older translations say *neglect* salvation. Many people would not openly *reject* salvation. They want it, in fact! But they *neglect* it by ignoring the means of God's grace. Is Esau an example of such an attitude? How can such a spiritual indifference show up in Christian churches, and how can we address this as Christians?

Lesson 5

The Lord Awakens Jacob to His Covenant Calling

Read Genesis 28:10–22

Introduction

Jacob must flee from his own home because his brother Esau is plotting to kill him. He leaves with only his staff in hand. But he also leaves with something very significant, namely, his father's blessing and his directives to find a wife among his relatives in Paddan-Aram (Gen. 28:2ff.). This story in verses 10–22 begins then with this flight away from his family, and it will end with a reference to a safe return to this same family. Jacob will receive more than his father's blessing: he will receive God's promises that will direct Jacob's life in the covenant of grace. Jacob will be gone for twenty years (Gen. 31:38). It is likely that his mother Rebekah dies before his return (cf. Gen. 35:8).

"He reached a certain place . . ." (28:10–11)

Jacob sets out on a journey without the benefit of any trains, planes, or automobiles. Beersheba is the point of departure, a place in the southern part of Canaan, and he heads north to his relatives at Haran in Paddan-Aram, near the northern point of the Fertile Crescent. This was a journey of about 500 miles (800 kilometers), almost certainly on foot (Gen. 29:1 says literally that he "lifted his feet"). The spot where he stops is over 50 miles (over 80 kilometers) from Beersheba.

The Life of Jacob

This stop is not named, interestingly, until the end of the story. It is only called a "certain place." The word "place" will be used six times in this story. Of course, this place to stop in order to rest for the night is not a place chosen by chance in God's plan: the LORD remains in full control of the events in this story.

Sights and sounds in Jacob's dream (28:12-15)

The sun has set, and Jacob stops for the night. This sets us up for the kind of event that has happened before.
In Genesis 15, God had appeared to Abram as a burning torch and smoky oven. God made great unconditional promises to Abram that concerned the central pillar promises of the covenant of grace. God holds before His people these key promises: land and seed (descendants). Now in Genesis 28:12ff., Jacob has a dream. God is going to reveal more of Himself to this fleeing patriarch.

What does Jacob see in his dream? Some translations say that it was a "ladder" that reached between heaven and earth. Other translations are certainly closer to the picture seen in the dream when they translate the word as a stairway or a kind of staircase. In the ancient world people might build an artificial "mountain" and at the top would be a temple or shrine to the gods or goddesses they worshiped. These constructed "mountains" with a staircase were called *ziggurats*. Steps or stairways would allow the priests and worshipers to ascend to the top and down again. This kind of structure is likely what Jacob sees in this dream.

Besides this structure that connects earth and heaven, Jacob sees angels going up and coming down on the stairway. They descend on "it," which can be interpreted to mean on "him," i.e., on Jacob. Angels are messengers, created beings that inhabit the corridors of heaven, always ready to do the will of God. The book of Revelation pictures heaven as occupied by many creatures, and many

The Lord Awakens Jacob to His Covenant Calling

of those creatures are the angels who join together with the saints in praise to God Almighty and to the Lamb.

The angels in this dream are likely shown to be the fellowship link between Jacob on earth and the LORD God in heaven. Divine revelation will make its way to Jacob, even as his own situation and concerns will be known to the Father in heaven.

But the most important character in the dream is the LORD Himself. He is standing at the very top of the stairway, and thus He is the central focus of the dream. We may very well understand that God is standing over "him," i.e., over Jacob. He watches over His people, day and night (Ps. 121). But more important at this point than His appearance is the short speech that the LORD gives to Jacob. In His word of address, God draws attention to the following important items:

1. He is the "God of your father Abraham and the God of Isaac." He is the God who maintains His covenant relationship through the generations of His people.

The God of Abraham and Isaac has "caught up," one might say, with Jacob.

2. The land on which Jacob now sleeps will belong some day to Jacob's descendants. Remember, Jacob is not yet married, and the LORD is talking about children!

3. In fact, the children will be numerous, and they will spread out in all directions.

4. All nations will be blessed through Jacob's family.

5. God will be with Jacob always. Here is the "immanuel" promise: God will be with His people.

6. God will protect Jacob wherever he goes.

Count your many blessings, Jacob! God promises Himself, land, children, blessing, and protection. Is Jacob merely dreaming all this? Can God deliver on what He promises?

The Life of Jacob

Jacob responds to divine revelation (28:16–22)

That's it! The dream ends, but Jacob has now been awakened to divine realities in the covenant of grace that God makes with His people. How will he respond to what he has seen and heard in this amazing dream of the night? Jacob responds with both words and works, with both fear and a vow. First, he notes that LORD is in this place but he (Jacob) was not aware of it. This is an interesting statement if we might, for a moment, place it against the background of some pagan beliefs of that day and age. Some say that the ancient peoples believed that if you slept in a sacred place and had a dream there, that you could induce or almost force the god or goddess to reveal himself or herself at that spot. Jacob came and stopped at "a certain place" (v. 11), but we do not get the impression that Jacob was trying to coax God to reveal Himself to him. In fact, quite the opposite! Jacob says in verse 16, "Surely the LORD is in this place, and I was not aware of it." Jacob was not looking for God in particular, so God came to him, even when Jacob was not expecting it. God chose to be here that night because Jacob was there in God's providence. In the biblical text, this is the first direct encounter between God and Jacob. But it will not be their last meeting!

Second, as the thought of encountering God in this place sinks into Jacob's heart and soul, he is struck with fear (v. 17). No wonder! This is the great God who created all things by the Word of His power, the God who is a consuming fire, unable even to look upon sin. Can anyone see God and live?

Third, we note that God has obligated Himself to Jacob, but curiously, the LORD has not explicitly demanded anything from Jacob. This does not mean that he can live in any way he pleases. God's people are always required to live holy and blameless lives. But the events of Genesis 27 have not particularly shown any of Isaac's family members as

The Lord Awakens Jacob to His Covenant Calling

especially attractive, and Jacob's deception of his father hardly shows him to a kingly-priestly type of character. Yet it is quite striking that God's revelation (first) to Jacob draws out of him several other reactions.

Jacob draws attention to the awesomeness of this place. This will lead to the place receiving the name that is the most familiar to Bible readers: Bethel ("house of God"). God's revelation causes a name change (so common in biblical revelation, isn't it). What is more, Jacob declares that this place is the "gate of heaven" (v. 17). When we turn back to the story of the Tower of Babel in Genesis 11, we find similar ideas but coming from the wrong direction. At Babel, man wanted to make a name for himself, so he built a towering city, a highway to heaven, a stairway to the stars. But God broke up that wicked, humanistic program with a confusion of man's languages so that later in redemptive history He might unite all nations in Jesus Christ, in His church, through the preaching of the holy gospel, in the power of the Holy Spirit. At Bethel, God reached down to Jacob, so that he might respond in faith.

Jacob anoints his pillow of stone. This was an act of consecration. Something that has been anointed is now holy, marked as separate from ordinary use and given over to God. In the Old Testament both people (e.g., kings, priests) and physical objects are anointed. This stone pillar, now set apart, is a kind of prophecy of a time when the land of Canaan will be set apart and occupied by God's people fully, as now in the New Testament era, God's holy people are called to fill the whole earth and dedicate everything in life to the LORD God of heaven and earth (see Zech. 14:21–22; Matt. 28:16–20).

Jacob also makes a vow. The word "if" in verse 20 can also be understood as "since." Jacob is not so much doubting God's word of promise so much as he is setting before Him the realities of what is in the future. After all,

The Life of Jacob

what does Jacob have in his own hand? His staff! But the future in God's covenant is rich in its prospects. God says that He will be with Jacob, but only time will tell. God is always true to His Word, but Jacob must see this for himself. Amazingly to him and to us all, Jacob will see the promises fleshed out. The LORD will be His God, and this is what Jacob will confess as he approaches his own death.

Jacob also vows to give to God a tenth of all he will receive from God. This statement at the end of verse 22 is significant because in it Jacob confesses that what he will receive will be a gift from God. God's generous revelation has now stirred up in Jacob an awareness that the birthright and the blessing will be significant for the coming of the Kingdom of God. Jacob has received much in the birthright and the blessing, and God has promised him much. But to whom much is given, much is required.

As beautiful as Jacob's reaction is to this event and to this place, the Israelites would later introduce corruption in their worship here and elsewhere. For example, Jacob sets up his stone pillow and anoints it as a consecration spot to the Lord. But superstitious Israelites would later set up such pillars as images of idolatry. Deuteronomy 16:21–22 says, "Do not set up any wooden Asherah pole beside the altar you build to the LORD your God, and do not erect a sacred stone, for these the LORD your God hates" (cf. Exod. 23:24; 34:13). Jeroboam I, first king of a divided Israel, would set up golden calves at Bethel in order to keep the northern Israelites from traveling to Jerusalem and worshiping at the Temple. How easy it is for our wicked hearts to manufacture idols and to corrupt the pure worship of God. Superstition about things and places is still with us, even with people who call themselves "Christians."

The Lord Awakens Jacob to His Covenant Calling

Ascending and descending on the Son of Man

Read John 1:50–51. In this context Jesus has encountered Nathanael, who confesses that Jesus is the Son of God, the King of Israel. Jesus responds by telling him that he would see even greater things. Indeed they would see heaven opened with God's angels ascending and descending on the Son of Man, the title that Jesus typically uses in the Gospels to identify Himself. Jesus is drawing upon the dream of Jacob at Bethel, but He drops any reference to a ladder or staircase. The "house of God" (Bethel) is the place where God and man meet to have true fellowship together. Jesus Christ is today that Person through whom God and sinful humanity are reconciled. He alone is our Mediator, whose cross on Good Friday points to the true and only way to heaven. There is no more need for an earthly Temple composed of gold, stone, wood and veils. Christ has opened Paradise for all God's elect through His death on the cross and His resurrection from the dead.

Thus Jesus' words in John 1:50–51 reveal that the great honor given by the Jews to the patriarch Jacob must truly shift to Jesus Himself. It is in Jesus that divine revelation has become flesh to dwell among us (cf. John 1:14). He is the true Temple for His people. Only Christ is the "gate of heaven" (cf. John 14:6).

Conclusion

Jacob was running for his life. He was not looking for God. But God came to look for him by means of a dream. In this way Jacob is awakened to new realities, made aware of promises that God will keep in order to restore all things to Himself again. Jacob and his family (yet to be) will have important responsibilities in that great redemptive plan. But in order to move forward by faith, God must put His promises underneath Jacob's feet. Therefore, what God does on that night by that "certain place" which becomes Bethel, is good news—for Jacob and for us who read this story of grace.

Lesson 5: Points to ponder and discuss
1. Read Genesis 15 again. What does God promise specifically to Abram? God makes a covenant with Abram, but the language literally says that God "cut a covenant" with Abram. What does that mean in Genesis 15? How does Abram respond to God's promises?
2. Look up the word "angel" in a Bible dictionary or Bible encyclopedia. What does the Bible teach us about the role of angels in God's world?
3. Read Isaiah 6. What are the similarities and differences that Isaiah experiences when he sees the Lord "seated high and lifted up," compared to Jacob's dream?
4. There are other people who meet the LORD or His Angel. Can you name these people? How do they react when meeting Him? What do they say and do? For starters, see Exodus 3:1ff.; 24:10, 11; 33:12ff.; Judges 13; etc.
5. We sing in one great hymn, "How vast the benefits divine that we in Christ possess." What were the benefits that Jacob possessed by the end of Genesis 28? How do these relate to what Christians today have in the finished work of Jesus Christ?
6. Jacob says that he will give a tenth to the LORD. How is this also an act of faith in God? How is all giving to the work of the LORD supposed to be an act of faith for us today?

Lesson 6

Jacob Marries the Mothers of Israel

Read Genesis 29:1-30

Introduction

Jacob has traveled the great distance from his parents' lodging in southern Canaan to the region of Paddan-Aram. The LORD came looking for Jacob, and He revealed His covenant promises to Jacob by means of a dream at the place that is renamed Bethel ("house of God"). Jacob hears for himself the covenant promises of God, and he responds in faith with a vow to serve the LORD God in the future.

Meeting at the watering-hole (29:1-12)

Jacob can now continue his journey to his relatives, to "the land of the eastern peoples." We remember in our reading of Genesis of another arrival there in an earlier chapter. In Genesis 24 Abraham had sent his servant to this region to look for a wife for his son Isaac. The issue then is the same issue now for Jacob (at least in part), namely, the wife must be from the same larger clan and thus (presumably) from the same faith. But there is something that is quite different: Abraham's servant goes with ten camels and "all kinds of good things" (Gen. 24:10). Abraham wanted to impress the potential bride for Isaac (and the bride's family) with his wealth, presumably a bridal gift. But what does Jacob have in his hand when he arrives at the local well? He has his staff. In other words, he is virtually empty-handed when it comes to the physical things of this world.

47

The Life of Jacob

Jacob heads to the local watering hole where people would bring their flocks for a drink of water. It is remarkable that this kind of story in the Bible is almost a kind of "type scene," the kind of story that is repeated at several points to indicate where a man meets the woman whom he would marry. We have already referred to Genesis 24, where Abraham's servant travels to obtain a wife for Isaac, Abraham's son. He comes to a well (Gen. 24:11). Moses also meets his future wife at a local watering hole in Exodus 2:15ff. We see the pattern: 1) a man travels and stops at a well; 2) a girl (or girls) comes along to get water for her flocks; 3) the man introduces himself, often by drawing water for the flocks; 4) the girl informs her parents of the man; 5) the man is brought to her home; and 6) a marriage is then arranged.

Jacob actually tries to get the shepherds to move along, to leave the site of the well since they have told him that Rachel, Laban's daughter, is making her way to this well. "It's the middle of the day. This is not the time to water the flocks," Jacob says to them in verse 7. "Get back to work . . . in the fields!" in other words. Apparently Jacob wants his meeting with Rachel to be relatively private.

The well is covered by a large stone. This is obviously done in order to prevent excessive amounts of dirt, filth, and garbage from falling into the water, thus polluting it. A large stone covering may also have been a safety feature, used to keep a person (perhaps a child) or an animal from falling into it, especially at night. It may also be in order to restrict its use to the local residents. Outsiders perhaps may have been required to pay for the use of the well.

The shepherds would have to work to roll this large stone away to use the well, and then roll it back in place. Some stones in these situations might require two or three men to remove them in order to get the needed water.

Verse 3 notes that the shepherds (plural) were the ones

Jacob Marries the Mothers of Israel

who rolled this stone away, but in verse 10 the text says that Jacob alone rolled it away. Not bad for a man in his late 70s! He experiences a surge of strength that enables him to perform this particular feat. We think of the strength of Samson later on, when the Spirit comes upon Samson to enable him to carry out his warfare against the Philistines. Apparently the shepherds are still hanging around and witness this act of great strength (see v. 9).

But more importantly, these shepherds show no hostility to this recently arrived stranger. In fact, they know Jacob's uncle Laban and that he is doing well (v. 6). God's providence is clearly in evidence here in this encounter at the watering hole. At Bethel earlier God had promised to be with Jacob (Gen. 28:15), and here is a meeting that shows God to be true to His word. There are no chance encounters or accidental meetings. God is working out the events so that He might advance His plans in Jesus Christ. Jacob had fled Esau to escape being murdered, but God has bigger things in mind for His Kingdom in Christ.

A further example of God's timing and arrangement of meetings here is the fact that at this very moment, while Jacob is talking with the shepherds, Rachel is coming along with the sheep. Here comes his cousin Rachel, a woman whom he probably had never met before in his whole life. She is in charge of her father's sheep, since in that culture, care for sheep might be handled by either a man (e.g., Moses, David) or a woman. Jacob proves himself quite useful as it is he who "puts his shoulder to the stone," so to speak, removes it and proceeds to water the flock. Whereas Jacob has been in a conversation with the shepherds, the text does not report any conversation (at least not yet) between Jacob and Rachel. Jacob acts, he works, and once he has finished watering the sheep, he kisses his cousin and breaks down in tears.

Why the tears? What is it that releases such emotion in

The Life of Jacob

Jacob? Perhaps it has struck him deep in his soul to see the coming together of so many providences from the LORD. His original reason to flee his own home was to escape his murder-plotting brother Esau. The story about getting a wife was a useful cover story. But then God steps directly into the picture via the dramatic dream at Bethel. "I will be with you wherever you go," the LORD had promised Jacob. And who else but the LORD could have brought Jacob to this particular well at this particular moment when his own cousin, Rachel, daughter of his own uncle Laban, was coming to the well?

Jacob explains who he is to Rachel (v. 12), and this sets her into motion to report this remarkable news to her father Laban. Jacob has found "family," or better put, God has guided his steps in such a way that this man now finds himself in the midst of his own people. Many English translations do not bring this out so clearly, but in the original text there is the frequent use of the word "brother." See, for example, verses 4, 10, and 12. On one level, the word "brother" may simply be a term of general friendship; in Genesis 29 it has even stronger connotations. Read verses 4–12 and see how many times a word or phrase of family relationship is used. God truly is putting this solitary figure Jacob into a new circle of family.

Meet the parents (29:13–20)

By the field well, Jacob had kissed Rachel. But when Laban hears this news from his daughter Rachel that this relative Jacob has arrived in the area from such a great distance away, he appears to drop everything in order to run out to meet Jacob. We read in verse 13 that he "embraced him and kissed him," immediately showing his own emotional acceptance of Jacob and happiness at his arrival. This is an embrace of a family member as Laban says literally to Jacob, "Indeed you are my bone and my flesh" (v. 14).

Jacob Marries the Mothers of Israel

In verse 13 we read that Jacob told Laban "all these things." Everything? Did Jacob tell Laban that he had followed his mother's directions (remember: Rebekah is Laban's sister) in order to mislead his father Isaac and take the blessing away from his twin brother Esau? Or, did Jacob say that he's now here in Paddan-Aram in order to find a proper wife? If that is the story, Laban may very well have wondered what the bride-price was that Jacob had to offer. After all, Jacob is really empty-handed at this point. Would Jacob have traveled all this way to get a bride, but his wallet is empty, so to speak? The text leaves us with some questions at this point: what was the whole story that Jacob told to Laban? And how does Laban react?

A month passes, and Laban has an idea about how the relationship with Jacob might be brought into line. We must also admit that we are not exactly sure about the nature of the relationship that develops between Laban and Jacob. By saying to Jacob that he is "my bone and my flesh" ("flesh and blood"), Laban uses the language of blood relationship (v. 14; cf. Gen. 2:23; 37:27; etc.). Some scholars claim that a man with only daughters might adopt a male heir in order to keep his property in the family. Does Laban "adopt" Jacob as his own son? If so, we are surprised Jacob never calls Laban his "father," and Laban never calls Jacob his "son." In any case, Laban proposes paying Jacob for his work. And while we might be favorably inclined to receive a wage, does this perhaps reduce Jacob to the status of a hireling? What is Laban's game-plan in all this? Is there a hidden agenda at work here?

Meet your first wife . . . and second wife! (29:21–30)
Laban has two daughters, as Isaac has two sons. Just as Esau and Jacob differ from each other, so the daughters also differ, at least in appearance. We have read about the elder—younger sibling difference already in Genesis 25.

The Life of Jacob

Will something develop here along similar lines? Leah (her name means "cow") has delicate eyes, while Rachel (her name means "ewe") is beautiful in appearance. "Delicate" eyes need not mean that Leah has poor eyesight. It may mean that she does not have the dark eyes that many consider a feature of beauty. Jacob comes to love Rachel, the younger daughter, and he proposes to Uncle Laban that he work for seven years to acquire Rachel as his wife. Laban agrees, noting that it is good if such a marriage stays within the larger family circle. Better Jacob than some other man, reasons Laban. And Jacob's love for Rachel grows.

The seven-year engagement goes by quickly, and the day of the wedding arrives. This was an occasion of feasting and celebration, as weddings of two people in love should be. But evening comes, and darkness falls. Jacob takes his bride to bed; she is almost certainly veiled. Father of the bride Laban gives his maidservant Zilpah as a wedding gift to the newlyweds. Perhaps Jacob thinks, "It does not get better than this!"

But in the morning, Jacob wakes up to a new reality . . . and a different wife! What a surprise, even shock, for Jacob! After seven years of work, and it's Leah who is now his wife. Jacob had deceived his father, who could not see who was before him, and now the deceiver has been deceived when he could not see who his new bride is. But it is all legal and according to custom: Leah is now Jacob's lawfully wedded wife. In reading this we feel a bit scandalized by Laban's behavior, but for this wedding-night trick to succeed, both Leah and Rachel are playing along with it. We do not read of any protest from Rachel, for what happens here is not done in secret to her. In other words, the whole household of Laban is playing along with this, and therefore we can understand Jacob's morning-after outrage. "What is this you've done to me? . . . Why have you deceived me?" (v. 25).

Jacob Marries the Mothers of Israel

Laban gives Jacob a very lame answer. "Oh, sorry! Didn't I tell you that the oldest daughter must be married first before the younger one?" A deal is worked out: the wedding week celebration with Leah must be completed, and then Jacob may take Rachel as his second wife. But he must work another seven years to acquire Rachel as well. Very shrewd deal, indeed! Laban gets fourteen years of work from Jacob, marries two daughters off to a close relative (his own nephew), and Jacob has two wives, not just one. Aren't we all happy? But Jacob's love remains focused on Rachel, and the seeds of a new conflict have been planted.

Lesson 6: Points to ponder and discuss
1. Jacob happens to come to the well where the shepherds know Laban. Plus, Rachel soon arrives. We confess that nothing comes to us by chance (Heidelberg Catechism, Lord's Day 10). We think of Ruth happening to come to Boaz's field. What other incidents in the Bible have people and events "happen," but with important results? What events in your own life, perhaps, were significant as you look back upon them, but at the time seemed to be "chance" events?
2. Jacob meets his future wife Rachel at the field well. Jesus also encounters a woman in John 4. What different things does Jesus focus on in His conversation with this woman at the well? Jesus was not looking for a wife. Rather, He came to seek a spiritual "bride," the church. How does this connect with what Jesus does and says at the well in Samaria? What do we learn about the spiritual "bride" from John 4?
3. Laban appears in the story to be very thrilled at the arrival of his nephew Jacob. He embraced him, kissed

The Life of Jacob

him, and, in general, welcomed him into his home. Yet later events suggest that Laban will develop a kind of agenda in which he will "use" Jacob for his own ends. How is it possible for people to act lovingly and yet really be using people for selfish reasons? Do we always understand clearly our own motives? How is the love of God so different?

4. Jacob marries two women (sisters), and he acquires their maidservants as (secondary) wives as well. Does bigamy (or polygamy) violate a basic biblical principle regarding marriage? How would you argue your position from Scripture? Why do some Mormon sects still practice polygamy? What is the Mormon teaching on why polygamy is a "good" thing?

5. The people who had more than one wife in the Bible experience many things in terms of their several wives. Think of Solomon's 700 wives and 300 concubines! Who else in Scripture had many wives? Did that situation bring good, or did it bring distress and pain? Or sometimes both?

6. Laban's deception of Jacob in the matter of the brides recalls Jacob's deception of his own father Isaac in Genesis 27. What might God be teaching or showing to Jacob in this? Could these recent events be a sanctifying thing for Jacob?

Lesson 7

The Struggle for Covenant Children

Read Genesis 29:31–30:24

Introduction

God's providence led Jacob to his relatives in Paddan-Aram. He comes to a well where the shepherds know his uncle Laban, then his lovely cousin Rachel "just happens" to come along, and soon Jacob is integrated into the household of Laban. Jacob comes to love Rachel. Laban has had other plans for Jacob, and he deceives Jacob into marrying Leah, the eldest daughter, before he can marry his beloved Rachel. In addition, Laban gets Jacob to agree to work for a total of fourteen years, which is a remarkable agreement. Yet Jacob loves Rachel, and he accepts this arrangement.

God loves Jacob, but Jacob hates Leah?

We have referred to God's providence in bringing so many good things together for Jacob. The LORD does keep His word, although the twists and turns of life may not always be what we expect as He brings His promises into reality. In the events of Genesis 29, we have not read explicitly of God being involved, and yet we know all things are "working together for the good" of those who love God, for those who are called according to His purpose (cf. Rom. 8:28). The God who stood "at the top" of the stairway in the dream, over "it/him" (Jacob?), is also the same God who promised to go with Jacob. He is always the "God who is with us," His people.

55

The Life of Jacob

The text of Scripture now mentions God again, and the reference is to Leah and the birth of children (v. 31ff.). The LORD takes note that Leah was "unloved." The word used here is often translated as "hated," the same verb used, for example, in Malachi 1:2–3: "Jacob have I loved, but Esau have I *hated*." Jacob "hates" Leah, and that sounds rather jarring. What does this mean?

First of all, remember what is said in verse 30. He loves Rachel *more than* Leah. That helps to put the words of verse 31 in context. The very fact that the LORD gave Leah four sons (by the end of this chapter) means that she and Jacob were sexually intimate in order that such children might be conceived and then born. At least it is not the case that Jacob and Leah will have nothing to do with each other! If "to love" and "to hate" are opposites, perhaps we can understand such hatred on the part of Jacob toward Leah, if we understand consider what love means.

The word meaning *love* in the Old Testament can cover many things. It describes God's love toward Israel (cf. Mal. 1:2), our love as commanded toward God (Deut. 6:5), and even what Amnon felt toward his half-sister Tamar in II Samuel 13:1 (whom he "loved," but sexually assaulted!). The word *love* in the Old Testament may cover attitudes, emotions, and actions (or even combinations of all three!). When God loves His people, that reality does not exclude His anger at them from time to time because of their sin. Anger is not equal to hatred. An emotion (as a feeling) is not the same as an attitude or a commitment. Love from God indicates a firm commitment to seek His people's greater well-being, our ultimate good.

By the same token, the word *hate* may also cover attitudes, emotions, and actions (or combinations of these three). Jacob *hates* Leah, but this does not necessarily mean that he was physically abusive, verbally mean, or had dark, cruel thoughts toward Leah. He is married to her, but their

The Struggle For Covenant Children

relationship is nothing special, and it is likely that there is nothing overly warm and friendly in their dealings together. Jacob's attention and affection is to the far more beautiful and attractive younger sister/wife, Rachel. Perhaps Jacob basically ignores Leah, paying no attention to her presence, her thoughts, or her feelings. This kind of hatred (cool indifference) is certainly felt deep in the heart and soul of Leah.

Leah: a vine made fruitful by the LORD (29:31–35)
The LORD notices all this in Jacob's home. And Leah realizes this as well, as we hear what she says when she names her sons. God's compassion is clearly in evidence in that He will make her a fruitful vine in the household of Jacob. To have two wives is bigamy, and that is not God's ideal for marriage. For Jacob's household things are complicated by his love for Rachel over against Leah. God compensates for this, so to speak, by blessing Leah with children. In all she is the mother of six sons, plus a daughter named Dinah.

There are several striking things to notice in the naming of these children. First of all, we read that it is Leah who names the boys. We wonder: is Jacob so uninterested in the birth of children to his "hated" wife that he is absent when it comes time to name them? Secondly, Leah provides a kind of explanation for each name, and that is included in the Biblical text for the names of all the sons.
1. Reuben: "Notice, a son!" (or, He has seen my misery) Genesis 29:32
2. Simeon: "hears" Genesis 29:33
3. Levi: sounds like "attached"? Genesis 29:34
4. Judah: sounds like "praise" Genesis 29:35

Leah's words are remarkable in that with several sons she mentions the Name of the LORD explicitly (Reuben, Simeon, and Judah). She refers to God again when Issachar (sounds like "reward," Gen. 30:17–18) and Zebulun

The Life of Jacob

("honor," Gen. 30:19–20) are born later on. Leah acknowledges that the LORD God has given her these children. Whether Jacob is greatly pleased with such sons or not at this point, we may not know. But Leah confesses that it was God who blessed her with sons.

At the same time, there is a darker, even disturbing, side to her comments with the birth of her sons. Look again at her words when they are born. With several of her sons (e.g., Reuben, Levi, Issachar, Zebulun) she makes comments that express her hope that maybe now her husband Jacob will love her. Children born to Leah are God's blessing, but they become viewed almost as presents or gifts to win over an unloving husband. We can hear a quiet desperation, maybe a painful frustration, in Leah's words when another son is born, "Maybe, possibly, this son will finally win my husband over." But we never read that it is so.

"Warring" wives (30:1–13)

Rachel's natural instinct towards motherhood is frustrated by her infertility. She can see on a daily basis her own sister's blessings in terms of the sons that God has given Leah. Can we speak of Rachel coveting her sister's children, not in the sense of stealing or kidnapping the boys, but in the sense of being so driven, that she will resort to almost anything to have a son? To her husband she cries out, "Give me children, or I'll die!" (Gen. 30:1). But Jacob is not God. Some have noted a kind of irony in her words as they are a kind of veiled prophecy. Rachel wanted either children or death, and it will be in giving birth to her second son Benjamin, that she herself will die (see Gen. 35:16–19).

Rachel is loved by Jacob, and yet she remains a barren wife. Now begins the "war of the wives" when Rachel gives her servant Bilhah to Jacob. Something similar had happened earlier in the household of Abram and Sarah (Gen. 16). The barren Sarah gives her Egyptian maidservant

The Struggle For Covenant Children

Hagar to Abram in the hope that the servant would bear a son, and the child would be adopted as the son of the couple. There is this difference, however: Jacob already has four sons, and thus, he is not childless.

Yet Rachel's desire for a child is so great, that she will use her servant girl Bilhah to have children. We assume that Rachel will get the "credit" for any child to be born. This is what Rachel says in verse 3, "Sleep with her so that she can bear children for me and that through her I too can build a family." Rachel is prepared to use her handmaiden for her own purposes. The maidservant will become a wife for Jacob, but she will be a wife of secondary rank, a kind of concubine. Bilhah bears two sons: Dan ("he has vindicated, judged;" Gen. 30:4–6) and Naphtali ("my struggle;" Gen. 30:7–8). But the text does not give either Rachel or Bilhah the credit for the children. In Genesis 30:5 and 7 the text tells us that Bilhah bears sons *for Jacob*. Rachel thinks that she has a fighting chance, so to speak, in the "war of the wives" to even the score with Leah. But the text tells us that the covenant sons belong to the elect son, Jacob.

It becomes apparent that Rachel stops bearing children for a period of time. So then it is Leah's turn to make a counter move in this "war of the wives" when she gives her servant girl Zilpah to Jacob as well. Zilpah bears two sons: Gad ("good fortune" or "troop"; Gen. 30:10–11) and Asher ("blessed" or "happy"; Gen. 30:12–13). But even here again, the text points out to us readers in verses 10 and 12 that the sons born to Zilpah are *Jacob's*. If anyone is keeping score in this tragic-comic contest, then it is Leah with six sons, while Rachel gets credit for two sons. In the end, it is Leah who will be the mother of the priestly and the royal tribes. Levi (3rd son) will become the ancestor of Israel's priests, while Judah (4th son) will be the ancestor of David, the messianic king, as well as of the Lord Jesus Christ Himself, the final Messianic King. But for the moment, while the wives are trying to outdo each other in the number of children born, it is Jacob the patriarch who is filling his household with the foundational layer of the Old Testament church community, through his two wives and their two maidservants.

This is a story of struggle, but now it is not between brothers, as we had read earlier in Genesis 25 and 27. This is a struggle between sisters, but who are also competing wives in one household. Fertility and barrenness have become issues, and even the children are drawn in to be used like weapons in the hands of the women. "Now my husband will love me, since I am fertile and can bear him sons," is Leah's thinking.

Rachel, in turn, resorts to some very questionable tactics in her desire to have a child. She makes a deal with sister (and fellow wife!) Leah to get the mandrakes, a plant that was thought to help make a woman fertile. Jacob had struck a deal earlier to get the birthright from brother Esau. Is this deal between the sisters similar to the deal that Jacob acquired with Esau in Genesis 25?

God remembers Rachel (30:22-24)

In the end, God does *remember* Rachel. "Remember" is an important word. It is used in Genesis 8:1, when Noah is in the ark during the flood. It is used again in Exodus 2:24, when the Israelites cry out to God in their great misery. God remembers His covenant with Abraham, Isaac, and Jacob. The word returns in I Samuel 1:19, when Hannah cries out in her distress of being barren. Our God keeps His covenant, and He always hears the cries of the needy, of those who turn to Him when their backs are to the wall, and we have nowhere else to turn. The Psalms remind us of that great truth. For God to remember does not mean that He forgot (as we humans can easily have the so-called "senior moments"). God remembers, and such a thought

The Struggle For Covenant Children

(if we may speak that way) is the prelude to Him taking specific action for His people.
    In remembering Rachel, God opens her womb. She had viewed her barrenness as a "disgrace" (v. 23), but God's mercy removes the barrenness and dispels the disgrace. Rachel's firstborn son is named Joseph, which name means "May He add." How shall we understand her comments at the naming? Is she saying, "How wonderful to have a child! May God give me another blessing like it." Or is Rachel saying, "One son is fine, but it is not enough. I want more children!" We might wonder whether this desire for children has become an all-consuming obsession.
    Twelve children (11 sons and a daughter, Dinah)! Truly Jacob has a full quiver. Many in modern society would look down on that number of children. But God is building His church, also through the means of covenant children born in the house of a believer. These sons will be the foundational patriarchs for the Old Testament church of God, namely, Israel.

Lesson 7: Points to ponder and discuss
1. The sixth commandment says, "You shall not kill (murder)." Read Heidelberg Catechism, Lord's Day 40 and Westminster Larger Catechism, Q/A 134–136. What is forbidden in this commandment includes also envy, hatred, and the desire for revenge. The essence of hatred is the wish to remove the neighbor from our life, getting rid of that person placed next to us by God. How can that desire to remove a neighbor be a "slow death" for such a person, without anyone ever shooting or stabbing that person? Does Leah sense that hatred? How does she cope with it?
2. Read Psalms 127 and 128. How do these Scriptures view covenant children in relationship to God, to the family

The Life of Jacob

itself, and also to the larger society? How do such views relate (in agreement or in disagreement) with Western society?
3. Read Genesis 1:26-28 and Matthew 28:18-20. Population experts tell us that for a society to replace itself numerically, a couple should have, on average, 2.11 children. In many countries, particularly in Europe and in parts of North America, the birthrate has dropped below that number. At the same time, among Muslims (and others) the birthrate is higher than 2.11 children per couple. What will be the long-term effect if such birthrates continue? Is overpopulation also a possibility to consider? How should Christians view the mandate to "fill the earth" with Christian disciples?
4. "God moves in a mysterious way, His wonders to perform!" What is the irony here with regard to Leah and her children? Had Jacob wanted to marry Leah? What is his attitude toward her? What is Leah's importance in the coming of the Kingdom of God through her sons Levi and Judah?
5. Jacob is a polygamist, and this is not God's design for marriage. What kinds of tensions existed in this household? What must it have been like for these children to grow up in such a household? How can our homes create an atmosphere in which the covenant children sense in their hearts and souls that they belong to God?

Lesson 8

Jacob Aquires Great Wealth

Read Genesis 30:25-43

Introduction
The covenant promise had been that God would be with His people, He would create *seed* (people, a nation) and provide *land* (place to call home) for that seed. But He had also promised to increase the blessings that His people would receive. That was Isaac's blessing to his son in Genesis 27. God has enabled Jacob to acquire a goodly number of children through his two wives and their two maidservants. So is it now time for Jacob to gather his family together and move on?

Jacob asks for his family (30:25-26)
The agreement by which Jacob had acquired his wives required that he serve Laban for a total of fourteen years. Apparently those fourteen years are drawing to a close, and the birth of Joseph to beloved wife Rachel occurs near the end of those fourteen years. Laban had deceived Jacob at the wedding, and he has obtained a great amount of work and service from Jacob. Perhaps Jacob himself senses that he has been used, even taken advantage of by his wily uncle. Jacob now wants to depart from Paddan-Aram with his wife and children (vs. 25-26).

The very fact that he must ask for his own family now raises a new set of questions. Is Laban in such control of people that he has not really relinquished his two daughters to Jacob? If Jacob is truly married, then his wives, Leah and Rachel, are joined to him. One must always love and honor one's parents, as the 5th commandment requires. But in

The Life of Jacob

marriage a new social unit in the Kingdom of God has been established. Jacob has left his own father and mother, and he is married. He must cling to his wife (for him it is wives!) that God has brought into his life. Why must he ask Laban for his wives and children? Or, is Jacob simply being overly polite so that the departure from Laban will be on good terms and that there will be no hard feelings when Jacob and his large family set out on the way back to Canaan?

Another question that comes to mind here relates back to the plan that mother Rebekah had given to Jacob. "Go to Laban and wait 'a few days' until your brother Esau's anger has subsided, and I will send you word that it is safe to return here" (Gen. 27:43–45). In Genesis 30 we do not have any indication that Jacob has received that "all-clear signal" that it is safe to return to the family in Canaan. Yet Jacob in Genesis 30:25ff. seems eager to be on his way.

Jacob has received the following: God's promises, his wives, and his children. Now we read how the LORD increased his wealth in terms of flocks. But first, Jacob desires to depart from Laban, and he asks permission to leave. It appears that Laban has some kind of authority over his daughters. How much authority does Laban have over his two daughters (and their children)? Should a man like Jacob (who probably is in his early 90s by now) have to ask for his own family?

Laban renegotiates with Jacob (30:27–34)

Laban wants Jacob to stay. He is smart enough to realize that Jacob's presence is the source of riches for himself. The NIV in verse 27 says that Laban has learned by divination that his riches are the result of Jacob's presence. In other words, it pays to have Jacob around! The NIV footnote, however, suggests a different translation that does not include Laban's use of divination: "I have become rich (have prospered) and the LORD has blessed me because of

Jacob Aquires Great Wealth

you." This second possibility of translation thus leaves unanswered the question of whether or not Laban used divination, that is, any means of discovering knowledge apart from the revelation of God.

If Laban says that the LORD has given him many blessings, would that not suggest that Laban should submit himself fully to that same God? The true God is the source of all blessings. Psalm 104 tells us in a beautifully poetic way that all creatures look to God for their food. Daily bread on our tables as well as sufficient funds in our bank accounts are testimonies to the goodness of our heavenly Father. Prosperity should drive us to prayer, to thanksgiving and joyful obedience. Or, is formal godliness a means of gain, doing the "right things" in order to get something from God? Do we live with God in some kind of mercenary arrangement: we do something for God so that God might do nice things for us?

In any case, Laban gives credit for his good financial situation to having Jacob around. So in an effort to keep Jacob and his family nearby, Laban begins to talk about wages. "What can I pay you so that I can keep you here? Maybe I can pay you more." Jacob is useful to Laban for a good income.

Jacob also realizes this (vs. 29, 30). In responding to Uncle Laban, Jacob tells us that Laban had far less in terms of possessions when he had arrived about a decade and a half earlier. But that is quite changed now. The gross family income has gone up noticeably. Jacob, like Laban, also gives the LORD the credit for this surge in prosperity. Truly blessing comes from the LORD! But the time has come for Jacob to steer his own course with his family, now away from Laban. Jacob has been "used," and the time for that usage is now over.

Laban and Jacob strike a deal. A financial arrangement is made such that Jacob will receive all the speckled, spotted, and dark-colored sheep, and every spotted and speckled goat. Victor Hamilton (*Genesis 18–50*, pp. 282–283) points out that in the Mediterranean world most sheep are white and most goats are black. "Thus Jacob is requesting the irregular, abnormal parts of Laban's flock." The rest belong to Laban. Such animals will be obvious to the eye of any beholder. Thus, all things being equal, Jacob would have smaller flocks because he would have the animals that are not the "norm" in appearance. This is the deal to which they both agree (v. 34), and it is a deal in which Laban expected to prosper. Jacob's flock will consist of animals without spots or speckles, and the odds are not in his favor biologically for uni-colored animals to give birth to spotted, speckled, or dark-colored animals.

Jacob, "expert" in animal husbandry (30:35–42)

To achieve success, Laban separates the flocks with a three-day journey between them. This will make it virtually impossible for any mixing of the flocks. More than that, Laban takes away all the spotted and speckled (those with "white") male and female goats, placing these irregular animals in the care of his sons. By all these means Laban (whose name means "white") intends to frustrate any chance that Jacob would profit from this arrangement. But God is with Jacob, and that will be the decisive fact in all this. God had promised Jacob great things in His covenant promises (see Genesis 28:13–15), and God always keeps His word.

Jacob continues to work tending the rest of Laban's flocks (v. 36). This will be a critical factor, but not the most important one. Jacob makes a counter move, namely, placing striped branches in the water troughs, especially when the stronger females would come to drink. Apparently, some ancient people believed that what an animal saw before she gave birth would determine the look of the animal that was born. There is no scientific basis for this, and such a belief and practice strikes us as bordering on sympathetic magic, or what others would call "maternal impression." But does Jacob believe this? Possibly so, but this is not as clear as some commentators make it. In any case, there is something of a pun going on in this story. Laban means "white." Jacob takes some (white) poplar branches (with other branches), cuts white stripes in them, and he sets them before the female animals when they came to drink at the watering troughs. Jacob earlier got the best of Esau with "red" stuff (Edom means "red"). Now he is going to get the best of "whitey," i.e., his Uncle Laban!

At the same time, he also applies some very shrewd principles of animal husbandry when he placed such striped sticks in front of the stronger female animals (v. 41). Perhaps in his younger years, while twin brother Esau was off hunting animals, Jacob was learning animal husbandry with the flocks of his household, and maybe now he is applying that knowledge with telling effect. In the end, it is God who alone can give the increase and the blessing to Jacob's use of ancient "animal science," such that there is born a significant number of speckled and spotted animals, even to otherwise unspotted female animals. Laban's flocks are filling with weaker animals, while Jacob's animals are the stronger. But God had said back in Genesis 25:23 that the younger son would be stronger and would dominate. God is keeping His word, even in the area of livestock that Jacob was now getting. John Currid (*Genesis, vol. 2*, p. 102) is correct when he writes that "the effort expended by Jacob is not the means by which the results are gained. Success does not come by questionable ancient customs, but only by the hand of Yahweh." There is a miracle here! Whatever we may think of Jacob's methods, the text does not explicitly criticize him.

The Life of Jacob

And the bottom line is . . . (30:43)

In the end, what is God's intention here, since the increase in these sheep and goats in Jacob's flocks is God's doing? Can we detect the divine "hidden hand" in all this, and, if so, for what purpose?

This increase in Jacob's wealth must be connected with God's promises made earlier to the patriarchs Abraham and Isaac in Genesis. In Genesis 12:1–3 God had said that He would bless His people, even in physical ways, make them a blessing, and through them the nations would experience blessing. Abram's nephew Lot sees his own flocks increase as he is associated with Abram and his flocks (Gen. 13:5ff.). Genesis 15, 17, 22, and 26 give the patriarchs (and us the readers) repeated mentions of God's promises of blessing, specifically in terms of children and land. In Genesis 28:14 God tells Jacob in his dream at Bethel that his descendants will *spread out* in all directions (cf. Gen. 13:14–17).

Now here in Genesis 30:43 we read that "the man grew exceedingly prosperous," literally, "the man *spread out* strongly, strongly (or, very much, exceedingly)." We get a list of what Jacob owned during this new phase of his time with Uncle Laban: large flocks, all kinds of servants, camels, and donkeys. Earlier Abraham had entered Egypt during a time of famine, but he left a wealthier man (see Gen. 12:16–20). God is not afraid to bless His people, also in very physical ways. Just as Abraham will leave Egypt a richer man, despite his misleading of Pharaoh, so too Jacob will leave his semi-bondage state with Uncle Laban an incredibly rich man, in terms of his family and his flocks.

The covenant of God's sovereign grace continues to march on here. Jacob is not getting younger in this story, but he is getting richer. God has blessed him with a large family, and when Laban had tried to squeeze more works and longer service out of Jacob, God has blessed Jacob with larger flocks and great physical blessings. How this is all playing itself out in Jacob's heart and soul, is hard for us to determine. Time will tell as we await more of this story to play itself out.

Lesson 8: Points to ponder and discuss
1. Haran is not the Promised Land to which God had brought Abraham. How does God use and direct the circumstances that Jacob faced to make him want to desire to leave Laban and return to Canaan?
2. Jacob and Laban appear not to have had the best of relationships. We often joke about friction with our in-laws. Can such joking be overdone and even be needlessly cruel? What are several ways that we can be an encouragement to our extended family, without meddling and trying to control them?
3. Laban has "used" Jacob in several ways. Identify these ways. How easy is it also for us to use other people? When does such use become, in fact, abuse? Are we even always aware of what we are doing with other people? How does Philippians 2:1–5 point us to a different way in God's Kingdom?
4. What Jacob does with the animals leads to an increase in his own flocks, both in terms of quantity and quality of animals. Were Jacob's husbandry tactics an instance of wisdom, or of trickery, or of both? What does the text say? What is God's purpose here in increasing Jacob's flocks?
5. Read Psalm 144, especially verses 12–15. Is this a picture of God's blessings in the Kingdom of His Son, Jesus Christ? Does the Kingdom consist only in spiritual blessings, or are physical blessings also part of the picture? Are such blessings experienced in this life, or are we to look for such blessings only in the life to come?

The Life of Jacob

6. God often blesses His people with physical blessings. But read Hosea 13:4–6. What are the dangers to our own souls when we prosper? Are we able to focus on the things that really matter in God's Kingdom when we are "blessed" with success?

Lesson 9

The Lord Directs Jacob to Leave Laban

Read Genesis 31:1-55

Introduction
Jacob has been disadvantaged by Uncle Laban on several counts: he tricked Jacob at the time of the marriage so that Laban is able to get both daughters married to Jacob, and he gets fourteen years of work from a willing Jacob. Not bad for Laban! But God's "hidden hand" is also working out a great plan for this patriarch so that God's promises can be realized. Jacob is blessed with children in his tents and with increased livestock in his fields. In sum, God has kept His word to Jacob. The evidence is clear for all to see.

Restless relatives (31:1-3)
 Jacob detects that a different atmosphere has developed in the household of Laban. Even his cousins, Laban's sons, grumble against him as they see God blessing Jacob's flocks. Uncle Laban also appeared to become more and more alienated from Jacob. There is something of irony here: blessings from the LORD toward Jacob do not awaken rejoicing in Laban's household. Instead, bitter muttering begins to brew.
 We are reminded of something similar (not precisely the same, however) had happened between the herdsmen of Abram and the herdsmen of Lot in Genesis 13. While the situation with Jacob and Laban is not exactly like that of Abram and Lot earlier, one point of similarity between the two stories is that the divine blessing that is so clearly

The Life of Jacob

present with Jacob causes feelings of jealousy and suspicion in Laban's family. "Jacob has taken all that our father owned," say Laban's sons. This is no longer "one big happy family."

So there are human factors that are certainly at play in Jacob's decision to leave Laban. But more importantly, it is the LORD Himself who tells Jacob to leave. Mother Rebekah had told him that she would send word to him when it was safe to return home. But that word never comes. Therefore, it is the covenant God who will now move His son Jacob back to the Promised Land. Notice how the LORD describes Canaan: it is the land of *your fathers* (v. 3). Whereas Abram had come from Ur of the Chaldees in Mesopotamia, and this uncle with his family still live in Haran, Canaan is now viewed as the land of the ancestors. Even in the words that God uses, Canaan is home, the center, the place where Jacob really belongs.

Jacob rallies his wives (31:4–13)

Rather than go back to his home to speak with his two wives, Jacob summons them to the field where the flocks are (does he fear that someone—maybe a relative—might steal from him?). Leaving Laban and his family is no small matter. After all, Rachel and Leah are the daughters of Laban. Thus Jacob must persuade them that this separation is necessary. Jacob's speech is interesting in that he mentions some of the sore points in his relationship with his wives' father, Laban. But he also acknowledges that it was God who was the ultimate source of his prosperity. We further learn that Jacob has had another dream: an angel of God has told him to leave Paddan-Aram. The "God of Bethel" is now directing him to leave and return to his "native land" (v. 13). His speech points out human factors (father Laban has cheated him) and the decisive divine factor in his decision. "God told me to leave here and go back home."

The Lord Directs Jacob to Leave Laban

The wives "stand by their man" (31:14–16)
It is important that Jacob have his wives on his side in this struggle with Laban. We readers may wonder how Rachel and Leah will respond. After all, Jacob has not spoken too favorably about their father. Whose side will they be on? But in their response it becomes clear that they are loyal to Jacob, no longer tied to their own father Laban.

Their comments reveal to us that not only has Laban tried to use Jacob for his own purposes, but he has also taken advantage of his own daughters. "Our father has treated us as foreigners, and he has certainly eaten up our inheritance!" they say. They even say that he has "sold" them. So they urge Jacob to obey God.

Jacob and his household make their exodus (31:17–21)
Jacob had, by the grace and favor of God, become a wealthy man. He has many children, servants, and livestock. Anyone who has had to move from one home to another home can begin to appreciate something of the preparations and detail that go into the act of moving. Jacob is running away; he is fleeing (vs. 20, 21). Therefore, he must move quickly, lest his preparations for moving become known to someone from Laban's household. Even then, once Jacob and his large household actually leave, they must move quickly. Travel on camel can go relatively quickly, but to move livestock ahead quickly, is another matter all together. This flight is filled with danger, real danger and not imagined.

The remarkable thing here is that Rachel *steals* the teraphim, while Jacob *deceives* Laban by leaving without telling Laban. What were these teraphim? Check one or two Bible dictionaries. Laban later on calls them "gods" (v. 30). They could be small or large, and most scholars think of them as images of household gods. They are referred to in Judges 17:5; 18:14–20; I Samuel 19:13–16;

The Life of Jacob

II Kings 23:23–24; Ezekiel 21:21; Hosea 3:4; and Zechariah 10:2. Prophets denounced their use. The passage in I Samuel 19:13–16 is a rather humorous incident in which Michal, Saul's daughter and wife of David, uses these teraphim to trick her father's own messengers who have come to arrest David. Apparently they may have been large enough to be placed in a bed to suggest that a human being was under the bed covers! These teraphim may have identified who had inheritance rights to property. They may have functioned as a kind of deed to the property: the holder of the images is the owner of the property. If that is the case, then this is why Laban is so upset that they were missing. But what does that say about the religious practices in Laban's family? Or, is this "pay back time" for Rachel against her father, since Rachel and her sister Leah believe that they have been cheated out of property inheritance by their father (see vs. 15, 16)? Rachel's motives may not be completely clear to us. Still, what were idolatrous images doing in this home in the first place?

Laban in hot pursuit (31:22–35)

Laban had been involved in sheep-shearing, and therefore he is not in the immediate area when Jacob flees. To move such a large household could not have been a quick affair, and yet it takes Laban and his force seven days to catch up with him, and by then Jacob and his family are in Gilead (about 350 miles distant). This is a great deal of distance made in a week's time!

But God is still in charge. By means of a dream He puts Laban on stern notice that he must not do anything to harm Jacob. "Watch your words, Laban!" And yet when Laban speaks, he pours forth words in questions that are angry and insistent? "What's this? Why . . . ?" It reminds us of similar questions in Genesis 3:13; 4:10; and 29:25. Laban, the uncle who has manipulated many things to his

The Lord Directs Jacob to Leave Laban

own advantage stands before God's chosen one, and he sputters out charges against Jacob, as if Laban is a prosecuting attorney.

Laban knows that he cannot do anything against Jacob, but he demands to search for his precious "gods," the teraphim. The readers can tense a bit, since we readers know something that Jacob does not know: the idols are in Rachel's saddle bag. But the readers' tension switches to a smile when we picture Rachel, claiming to be in her period of monthly impurity, sitting on the "gods"! To think that people actually believe that a creature could have divine powers! See Romans 1:18ff.

Jacob's angry response (31:36–42)

Laban has treated Jacob as a common thief, with accusations and property searches. Once it is clear that Laban's precious idols (the teraphim) are not found, Jacob then responds with great anger. We sense that much frustration has been building up over all these years. It is clear that God has kept His word to be with Jacob. He has thrown His protecting shield around him. Laban has enough fear of God that he takes seriously God's warning. Laban may use talk tough, but in the end he takes no hostile action against Jacob.

Covenant made to keep the peace (31:43–55)

Laban answers Jacob with words that sound like he must "get the last word in." He basically says, "I really don't care what you say or think, Jacob. This is *my* family, and these are my *animals*. All you see is mine" (v. 43). These are remarkable words: brazen, possessive, proud. Yet Laban is also realistic now, knowing that God has thrown a shield around Jacob and his household. Laban can protest all he wants, and he can demand all he likes, but he will not get this family and these animals back under his

The Life of Jacob

control. God is in control! No doubt Laban has in his mind the stern warning that the LORD gave him in the dream.

Laban then retreats to the next best thing: let's make a covenant. The terms of the covenant focus on the following things: 1) protection of Laban's daughters, lest Jacob prove unfaithful, and 2) prevention of hostility between Laban and Jacob. Laban still seems so self-centered ("Mine!"), and yet he makes a very interesting statement about God in terms of this situation. God is witness to all this, including the marriage of Jacob with Rachel and Leah. God will be the "unseen Seer" in all these events.

Take notice of the components of this personal covenant: there is a sacrifice, coupled with a vow, witnesses are present (God, first of all, and then a heap of stones), and then a concluding meal. In a far grander way, God binds Himself to His elect with the sacrifice of His Son, His Word (of promise), the witnesses of Himself and all creation, and meal of bread and wine to confirm in believers the truth that is placed before us in the gospel of the Lord Jesus Christ.

Conclusion

Genesis 31 marks the conclusion of an important chapter that was written by God in the history of the coming of the Kingdom of God. Sad events caused Jacob to flee from family in Canaan (Gen. 28), and now a sad situation causes Jacob to flee from his extended family in Paddan-Aram. Jacob, now in his 90s, seems to be a "man on the run." He has been blessed by the LORD, but God's blessings have provoked in Laban less than pure desires. Jacob's future and that of his family are not in this area. God's plan for His people at this point includes location in the Promised Land, and that is where God's Word and human events now direct Jacob. S.G. De Graaf (*Promise and Deliverance*, vol. 1, p. 207) says this:

"By His Word the LORD had separated Jacob and Laban,

The Lord Directs Jacob to Leave Laban

so that Jacob would live only for the Word of the LORD and await the fulfillment of the promise in Canaan. Events had to take this course for the sake of Christ, who is completely removed from the sinful life of the world. Since Jacob's separation was not complete, the cleansing of his house would have to continue later."

Lesson 9: Points to ponder and discuss
1. Rachel and Leah seem bitter toward their father (vs. 14–16). Can this be a proper motive for encouraging Jacob to leave Laban? What should be the believer's motivation when doing the will of God?
2. God is pleased to work His covenant plan through believing households, through families where He is believed and honored. Yet human families are not the ultimate since the Kingdom of God can "set father against son and mother against daughter." Rachel and Leah choose for Jacob (albeit with less than pure reasons; question #1 above). Believers' heart loyalty is to God and His Son Jesus Christ. How can such loyalty to God today affect families? At what point does a person make a break with his or her own family members because of the Christian faith? And, if a break must be made, what then could and should be our attitude toward non-Christian family members?
3. What parallels do you see between the flight of Jacob and his household from Laban, and that of the Israelites later from Egypt? What kind of situation are both groups leaving? What does God say and do that enables both groups to leave, even to escaping real dangers?
4. Rachel wants to keep the teraphim. What does the presence of these idols and their use suggest about the level of spirituality in Laban's family? Is Rachel

spiritually like Lot's wife who "looked back" when she should have spiritually "cleaned house" in the move away from Paddan-Aram?
5. God is a Witness, the unseen audience of One to all that is said and done. How should that reality control what is said at a profession of faith, at a wedding, in business dealings, and in courtroom trials? Read Heidelberg Catechism, Lord's Day 37, Q/A 102.

Lesson 10

Jacob Prepares to Meet His Brother Esau

Read Genesis 32:1–21

Introduction

One crisis with Laban has been averted; another looms ahead for Jacob with Esau. A covenant seals the deal between Jacob and Laban so that there may be peace between them and their descendants. "Good fences make good neighbors," it is said. But Esau is a new neighbor that is just over the Gilead horizon to the south. Esau was fiercely angry when we last met him in the text (Gen. 28). Are there still storm clouds in his heart and soul?

Heavenly and human messengers (32:1–8)

Jacob continues to move toward the place where he will encounter his twin brother Esau. Laban, his father-in-law, is headed back to his home (Gen. 31:55), but Esau is before him. Yet while Jacob is moving south, we read that "the angels of God met him" (Gen. 32:1). The last time that Jacob saw angels was in Genesis 28:12 when he spent the night at Bethel, and he dreamed of angels ascending and descending on the stairway that connected heaven and earth. We've come full circle. That dream had been a source of great comfort and encouragement to Jacob as he left the Promised Land with only his staff in hand. God promised him great blessings in His covenant.

Jacob is returning home in Genesis 32, but now he is a richer, more powerful man. Yet the question is this: what will be the attitude of Esau now after twenty years? Will the

The Life of Jacob

murderous intentions earlier have died away? Or, will Esau still bear a grudge so intensely that Jacob needs to fear for his life? In addition, if Esau still seeks to destroy Jacob, he will certainly want to destroy his family (or enslave them, or sell them), and confiscate his vast possessions.

Jacob interprets the presence of this band of angels as a positive sign, namely, that God was with him and would help to protect him. So he gives this place a name: "Mahanaim" (which means "Two Camps," God's camp and Jacob's camp). The word for "camp" in the original language can also mean "army." Is there ambiguity here? Could it be that God's "army" has arrived because there is going to be a battle? In Genesis 31 Laban's "camp/army" had come in pursuit of Jacob and his "camp," but bloodshed was averted. Laban went back in peace. Can peace be preserved between Jacob and Esau?

In any case, Jacob sends messengers ahead to meet Esau first before he himself will encounter him. Again, the original language catches the wordplay since the word for "angels" in verse 1 is the same word for "messengers" in verse 3. God sends His heavenly messengers to Jacob, and Jacob now sends his earthly messengers to Esau. He wants to soften Esau, if that be needed, and to sweeten his disposition before the actual meeting takes place.

Furthermore, as a strategic precaution, Jacob divides his one camp into "two camps." See verses 7 and 10. After all, if Esau should attack one group, then there will be time, he hopes, for the other group to make its escape (v. 8).

The messengers that Jacob sends have instructions on how they are to speak. It is an interesting picture that they are to paint to Esau once they meet him. On the one hand, Jacob refers in verse 4 to his brother as "my master Esau." As for himself, he calls himself, "your servant Jacob" (verses 5, 18). In the context of the ancient Near East, that is suggestive that Esau is the "head" while Jacob is the "tail" (see

Jacob Prepares to Meet His Brother Esau

Deut. 28:13, 44b), that Esau is the *lord,* but Jacob is the *slave.* This is not quite how Genesis 25:23 said it was going to be! So, Jacob is clearly humbling himself before Esau in language that is very politically polite.

On the other hand, he wants to include in the message to his brother the fact that he has gained so much wealth in the time he lived by Laban. What a list: donkeys, sheep, and goats, menservants and maidservants! What message does Jacob intend to send with this inventory list of livestock and people? Does Jacob want Esau to be impressed? It could very well be that Esau, if he is still seething with anger, might hear this list of goodies and it could make him covetous and quite desirous of getting his hands on all this wealth.

Jacob's messengers return to him with ominous news: Esau knows that Jacob is coming in his direction, and he is coming toward Jacob. But Esau is not alone: there are 400 men with him. The text in verse 6 leaves the reader with a question: are the 400 men an attack party? Or, is Esau coming in peace with a large continent of his forces in order to have a reunion party? Which is it?

Jacob is going to "play it safe." He is seized with great fear and distress, says verse 7. Now he carries out his safety net plan of dividing his camp into two groups with the hope that if there is a violent encounter with Esau, then at least part of his group can likely survive.

Jacob's first recorded prayer (32:9–12)

When Jacob had realized the presence of God "in that place" of Bethel, he had responded to the dream of the previous night with wonderment, fear, and with a vow to serve the LORD God if He carried out His promises. It was not a prayer that was addressed to God directly. Here in Genesis 32 we now have the first recorded prayer of Jacob. This is not to suggest that this is the first time that he ever

The Life of Jacob

prayed in his life. We simply are not given information on the prayer-life of this patriarch (as we are rarely given insight on the prayer-life of many Biblical characters!). In any case, review the various aspects that Jacob mentions in his desperate prayer to God:

1. He addresses the God of his ancestors, Abraham and Isaac. He is speaking to the one, true God.

2. He recalls something that God had said to him earlier, specifically, the fact that God is the One who had directed him to return to the Promised Land and to his family. Jacob recalls a bit of history.

3. He humbles himself: "I am unworthy of all the kindness and faithfulness You have shown your servant." His word for "unworthy" is literally, "I am the little one, the younger one." He was, after all, the younger of the twins born to Isaac and Rebekah. He adopts a lowly spirit in the presence of Almighty God.

4. He acknowledges that he has been blessed. From one walking staff . . . to two groups!

5. He presents his petition, "Spare me! I'm very afraid for myself, for my children and their mothers!"

6. He concludes by mentioning again God's covenantal promise to make his descendants like the sand of the sea (see Gen. 28:14; cf. Gen. 22:17).

This is really an awesome prayer! God often seems to whisper in our prosperity, but He shouts to us in our pain. We have no way of knowing how "close" Jacob was to God during the twenty years of living with Uncle Laban. He labored, and he prospered greatly. Did Jacob give God the thanks and the praise of this during those twenty years? We do not know. But now, as Esau approaches, Jacob is afraid of losing all that he has. Yet, because he has nowhere else to go, he turns to the covenant God, who is ever faithful, and Jacob reminds the LORD of what He has said Himself. "This was Your Word, O my God, and these

Jacob Prepares to Meet His Brother Esau

were Your promises!" God is working in Jacob, stirring up in him a proper and prayerful dependence upon his heavenly Father.

Gifts that Jacob keeps on giving (32:13–21)
It is interesting to note that this section begins and ends with a notice that Jacob spent the night there (vs. 13, 21). The wrestling with the "mysterious Stranger" will also occur at night. Jacob has not yet come into the daylight, one might say. That will come later. For now, he makes plans at night.

Jacob, ever resourceful, draws up a strategy to pacify Esau (v. 20). He wants to soothe his (possibly) hostile spirit with wave after wave of gifts. These are valuable gifts of various animals: 550 animals in total, of which 490 are female. The female animals are valuable, of course, because of the prospect of bearing more animals later on and thus increasing the owner's wealth.

We wonder: is Jacob feeling something of "guilt feelings" over having deceived his brother Esau in Genesis 27 by getting father Isaac to bless him? Is this a way to pay back his brother with something of the abundance that the LORD has showered upon him? Perhaps so. In any case, the gifts are on their way, headed to Esau. Time will tell whether Esau will accept them (and favorably), or, whether he will tell the messengers of Jacob to "return them to sender."

How different are God's gifts to us in Jesus Christ! We earn nothing, and we cannot merit any of God's blessings. All that we have is a freely given gift to us in Jesus Christ. The wage we earn is death because of our sins, both in terms of our actual deeds and the sinful nature we receive from the first Adam. Jacob is trying to win Esau's favor. But Christians are liberated from all attempts to placate God's justice, since God has dealt with all of our sinful deeds and sinful nature by pouring out His wrath in

The Life of Jacob

justice upon Christ on the cross. Therefore, Christians live in joyful thanksgiving, not in cringing terror before God (cf. Rom. 12:1ff.).

Lesson 10: Points to ponder and discuss
1. Read II Kings 6:8–17. Elisha is calm, even though Syrian armed forces have surrounded the village to capture him, because he knows that the angelic forces were present. Recall what Christ said in the Garden of Gethsemane about the legions of angels He had at His command. Do such angelic forces still surround believers today? How do Romans 8:31ff. and I John 4:4 relate to this?
2. Jacob is afraid of his brother Esau. Does he have good reason for this fear? Why or why not? So many times we hear people in the Bible being told, "Don't fear!" What are the reasons for fear in Christians' lives? Are there things that we should fear? What things should we never fear?
3. Some twenty years have passed since Esau and Jacob have faced each other. Is it possible that a person can harbor a grudge or nurse anger for at least two decades? What would be the point? Does Esau have a just cause, if he indeed is still angry? What does the Bible say on how Christians must handle anger? See Ephesians 4:26, 27, and 31.
4. How do you evaluate the various strategies Jacob uses to protect himself and his grand camp? We might well ask, "Where is Jacob's faith? If the heavenly messengers have come to protect Jacob and his camp, how trusting is Jacob, after all?" Is Jacob doing the human thing, "just to make sure"? "God is with me, but I've also got to be 'practical'"? On the other hand, is wise strategy wrong? After all, Jacob is not using his strategy as a substitute for God, for his prayer shows his full reliance upon God.

Jacob Prepares to Meet His Brother Esau

5. Read Genesis 32:12. Why does Jacob remind God of the promise to make his descendants abundant "like the sand of the sea, which cannot be counted"? Could it be because Jacob is holding onto the promises of Genesis 28? Does he fear that a violent attack from Esau could wipe out the covenant future (humanly speaking)? Abraham had a similar situation in Genesis 22, when God told Abraham to sacrifice his only son, his beloved son. How did Abraham face that test? See Hebrews 11:17–19.
6. Reflect on what Jacob was like before he had fled from Esau, and what Jacob is like now. How has he changed, if at all? How does God work in His people to mature and sanctify them in Christ through His Holy Spirit?

Lesson 11

Jacob Wrestles with a "Mysterious Stranger" at Peniel

Read Genesis 32:22–31

Introduction

Jacob faces his brother Esau who, he learns, is coming to meet Jacob with four hundred men. Jacob's response is typical of those who feel their back is to the wall: he becomes physically defensive, sends great gifts to Esau, but most importantly, he is thrown back to prayer to the living God. Jacob has nowhere else to go except to God. Only God has the words of everlasting life; only God has the power to save us alive.

Jacob is left alone (32:22–24a)

The action in this story occurs at night. The sun will rise at verse 31. But before the sun rises, Jacob will send all of his family ahead of him by crossing the fords of the Jabbok. This is identified as the Wadi Zerqa (Zarqa), a dry-stream bed in which water flows only during the rainy season. It is located over 20 miles (about 32 km) north of the Dead Sea on the east side of the Jordan River. In other words, Jacob stands at the edge of the Promised Land of Canaan, but he is not quite there yet.

Sending his family and all his possessions over this brook at night would be a very cumbersome and even dangerous venture. This is something that almost certainly could not be done without moonlight and torches. But once all are across the stream, we read that Jacob was "left alone" (v. 24a). It reminds us of the night spent 20 years earlier at

The Life of Jacob

Bethel when he was fleeing Esau and leaving the Promised Land. Once again Jacob, despite all his wealth in family and earthly goods, is totally vulnerable and defenseless.

Who is the Stranger in the night?
Jacob is not a young man anymore, and yet we read that he engages in a wrestling match until daybreak. But who is his wrestling opponent? The text gradually reveals the identity, and both the reader and Jacob himself eventually recognize who this "mysterious Stranger" is. By the time dawn breaks, it has dawned on us all who He is.

Yet in the history of interpretation there have been a variety of explanations. Nahum Sarna (*Genesis*, p. 228), a Jewish commentator, says that Jacob struggled with "the celestial patron of Esau"! Some commentators in the higher-critical tradition say that Jacob's opponent was a "Canaanite river god"! But what does Genesis 32 itself say? As the wrestling match begins, he is identified as a *man* (v. 24). But by daybreak, when the "man" tries to break off the match, the Stranger says that Jacob has wrestled with *God*. Jacob himself acknowledges this in verse 30 when he says that he had seen *God* face to face.

Read Hosea 12:2–5. There it says that he wrestled with an angel and prevailed. So the Scripture calls the "mysterious Stranger" a man, God, and an angel. We have met this kind of identification combinations before. Three strangers come to meet Abraham in Genesis 18, and one of them is the LORD Himself and the other two are angels. Later on in Joshua 5:13ff., Joshua will meet a "man" with a drawn sword, but he turns out to be the Commander of the armies of heaven, the LORD (cf. Joshua 6:1). In Judges 13, the "angel of God" is the "man of God." Many of these occasions are understood to be an appearance of the Lord Jesus Christ Himself, centuries before He is born in Bethlehem.

Jacob Wrestles with a "Mysterious Stranger" at Peniel

Jacob under attack?

One question that comes to mind is this: why does this divine Being wrestle with Jacob? Is He attacking him? Perhaps this suggests a later encounter in Exodus 4:24, where Moses is going back to Egypt, at the command of the LORD, but God "attacks" Moses, indeed He tries to kill Moses! Is the LORD trying to prevent Jacob from returning to Canaan? Or, is the wrestling a kind of test, one similar to the LORD's test of Abraham in Genesis 22, when He tells Abraham to sacrifice his only, beloved son? In the Bible to meet someone "face to face" can be an encounter that may be hostile, or it can be friendly. Is this just a "friendly wrestling match"?

Further head-scratching things come up later. If this being is divine, superhuman, an Old Testament appearing of Christ, then how do we understand verse 25, "When the man saw that he could not overpower him . . ."? Is this something that God could not do? Certainly if God is able to create all things by the power of His Word, surely He can defeat this elderly man, Jacob, even if he is in really good shape! God has come to Jacob in the form of a man, and He has even allowed Jacob to wrestle Him "successfully." This is an instance of God's merciful condescension: He comes down to our level to reveal something of Himself and of His purposes with mankind in the covenant of grace. But what is God revealing here?

At the same time, notice that Jacob has his hip dislocated (or made numb) by the simple touch of the Man's hand. This suggests the superhuman strength and power of the Stranger. The Stranger does not "win" the wrestling match, and yet He can apply a single touch and wrench Jacob's hip socket out of place.

Jacob asks a blessing . . . and gets a new name

The "mysterious Stranger" wants to break off the

The Life of Jacob

wrestling match as the dawn appears. It is not clear why He wishes to stop at that point. Perhaps it is because in the full light of the day, Jacob will "see" God, but that is a sure sentence of death. No one can see God and live.

Jacob has the strength to hold onto the Man. "I will not let you go unless you bless me!" To be sure, human beings in the Bible can bestow blessing, but certainly God alone can make any blessing effective. In any case, the greater blesses the lesser, and Jacob by now senses that he is holding onto a divine Person. Yet he is not so much afraid as he is bold to ask for the blessing. Jacob sees that only God can give him a blessing. No more tricks or human cleverness will work now.

Rather than immediately giving Jacob a blessing, the Stranger asks for his name. Jacob, the name based on the word for "heel," is his name. The Man says that his name will no longer be "Jacob," but it will be "Israel." Earlier God changed the name Abram ("exalted father") to Abraham (sounds like a "father of a multitude"), and Sarai becomes Sarah (both names mean "princess"). The new name indicates something of the place and purpose the person will have in the unfolding of God's redemptive program.

The name *Israel* means literally, "God struggles," but not in the sense that God has trouble getting to His goal. Rather, this new name points out the nature of living in the covenant with the true God. Jacob has indeed struggled with two sets of opponents: with God and with men (e.g., Esau, Laban). Yet Jacob has overcome. In all these struggles God has been with Jacob. This is what He promises His own whom He has always loved. God's presence with Jacob is not to endorse everything Jacob has done to other people. It is to carry him along so that God might establish a people of His own, so that they might be the light of the world, so that the Christ would come in our flesh.

Jacob wants to know the name of his wrestling opponent.

Jacob Wrestles with a "Mysterious Stranger" at Peniel

Fair is fair, after all: Jacob surrendered his name. Verse 29 reads, "Please tell me your name." But the Stranger will not give it. He grants a blessing, but He remains closed-lip about His own name. He will leave that night, before the day breaks, and Jacob will have no name by which he can identify the Man.

A blessing won at a price

The Man blessed Jacob (v. 29c), just as Jacob had wanted. But the blessing comes at a price: Jacob limps as he walks, for he has been wounded in his thigh. The Man has yielded nothing, not even His name. Jacob must learn something in this night of wrestling. He—and God's people today—must know that our covenant God is also tenacious, long-suffering, patient, to a people whose sins and sinful nature make them, in fact, worthy of eternal hell. God has committed Himself to His Word for the sake of the Christ and all the elect. Why does God even bother? The answer is because He has committed Himself to this, and it is all for His grace and glory. He will not break His Word. But that is the nature of divine, electing love.

Who won this wrestling match? If Jacob "won" against God, then meeting Esau will be no match at all! "If he has survived meeting God, he will survive his meeting with Esau" (Wenham, *Genesis 16–50,* p. 297). Now Jacob knows something, not so much about his strength, but he knows something about his God. This is reflected in the name that Jacob gives to the place. "Peniel" means "face of God," for Jacob makes a confession of faith, "I saw God face to face, and yet my life was spared." As the morning dawns, it dawns on him that the God who will wrestle with him all night, the God who can dislocate his hip, is the God who is not poised to destroy him. He is the God who is really on his side. He is, after all, Immanuel ("God is with us").

We have come full circle in a sense: when Jacob arrived at

The Life of Jacob

Bethel in Genesis 28, the sun set and it was night. Then the LORD God appeared to Jacob in a dream, and He gave him the promises of the covenant of grace. Twenty years of blessing pass. Now, in this chapter God comes at night as a Man to Jacob, blesses him especially in the gift of a new name. And now the sun rises over Jacob, renamed Israel, as he limps back to his family.

Lesson 11: Points to ponder and discuss
1. One commentator says that the "two most significant events in the life of Jacob were nocturnal theophanies," that is, God appears to him at night. The first was at Bethel (Gen. 28:10–22) and now here at Peniel. Each appearance (theophany) was life-changing. Why were these significant, and how were they life-changing?
2. Christ appears in the Old Testament before He is born at Bethlehem as the "Word made flesh." Some of those appearances were already mentioned in the lesson.
   Can you think of others in the Old Testament? Think of those places where the "Angel of the LORD" is mentioned.
3. Jacob will not let the Stranger go until He gives Jacob a blessing. Why does Jacob want this blessing? He has been blessed before by his father Isaac (Gen. 27), and God has not only promised blessings to him, but also delivered in terms of family and possessions. Does Jacob want a blessing simply to be successful in meeting Esau? If so, is this a true act of piety?
4. How do we receive God's blessings today? Why do we want His blessings—for ourselves, or for the coming of His Kingdom?

Jacob Wrestles with a "Mysterious Stranger" at Peniel

5. How, do you think, would Israelites hear and understand this story, especially what is revealed about the source of their national name? Why do we need to hear and meditate on this story today?
6. Sometimes Christians speak of periods of deep discouragement as the "dark night of the soul," a time of depression and setbacks. Are we really ever abandoned by God? How can our faith hold onto God? What role can the Christian community play for brothers and sisters who go through such a period of darkness and discouragement?
7. The holy Trinity is three Persons. The Father does not appear, and the Holy Spirit is like the wind (cf. John 3), whose effects we can experience, but whose Person we cannot see. The second Person of the Trinity appears from time to time, supremely in the birth of Jesus in Bethlehem. But what does John see of Christ when he sees Him in Revelation 1?

Lesson 12

Jacob and Esau Meet Again as Brothers

Read Genesis 33

Introduction

Jacob has met a "Mysterious Stranger," and they wrestled through the night. It becomes apparent that this Man is no ordinary human being. He gives to Jacob a new name—Israel—since he has struggled with God and won. Jacob has become the "winner" by sovereign permission and divine appointment. With this new name, this elect child of God now moves on in redemptive history. God has been with him during all these years of struggle, and God will continue to be with Israel (Jacob), even if He needs to struggle with him from time to time. The night of wrestling and struggle sets us up for the next great challenge that Jacob will face, namely, he must meet his twin brother Esau again. Jacob has met one Man; now he faces 400 men!

How good and pleasant is the sight . . . (33:1ff.)

During these past twenty years, it appears that Esau also has become powerful and successful. He has four hundred men with him. Jacob, for his part, divides his household into groups such that his beloved wife Rachel and son Joseph are last, placed in the safest part of the party. The maidservants with their children are the vanguard of the entire clan, with Leah and her children following afterward. In other words, the (presumably) least loved group goes first, with the best loved at the end. At the very least, Jacob is being cautious because he does not know in

The Life of Jacob

what mood or with what spirit his brother Esau is approaching him.

Jacob sets the tone for the meeting with Esau. He comes ahead of his family, showing at least external bravery, and he bows down seven times to his brother. One full prostration on the ground would have been enough in that culture, but seven times is a "perfect" demonstration of absolute submission and full honors to Esau. Earlier Jacob prayed for the LORD's help (Gen. 32:9–12), and he has recently wrestled with the divine Stranger at night, emerging with success. God is responding to His chosen "son" to increase his faith and confidence in a situation that is potentially deadly.

The text tells us in verse 4 that Esau *ran* to meet Jacob. Although both men are well on in years, Esau retains some physical vigor. Jacob is clearly at a physical disadvantage as he limps along. Here is where he must trust again upon the goodness and protection of God because Esau has the manpower to attack and devastate Jacob and his household.

The meeting goes much better than what Jacob had anticipated. Jacob's concerns appear to be groundless. It is indeed a tender moment after 20 years of separation. It reminds the student of the Scriptures of other tender moments of greeting: Joseph greets his brother Benjamin (Gen. 45:14) and later his father Jacob (Gen. 46:29). In the New Testament the father in the story of Luke 15:20 runs to meet his prodigal son, even after the son had left the father's house in a rather dishonorable manner. Family members meet each other with warm embraces and freely-flowing tears. We might well sing Psalm 133!

Notice the *words* and the *actions* of Jacob as he interacts with Esau. This is a fascinating study of how the two twin brothers relate at this reunion. Jacob refers to himself as "your servant" (see vs. 5, 14), while he calls Esau his "lord" (see vs. 8, 13, 14 [twice], and 15). In the ancient

Jacob and Esau Meet Again as Brothers

world, that kind of language suggests a relationship of superiority for the one, servanthood and humility for the other. At one level, it is designed to put Esau into a "kinder, gentler" mood, if he is in fact still harboring some of the anger and bitterness that he had two decades earlier.

Esau, on the other hand, addresses Jacob as his "brother" (v. 9). For Esau, it appears that he is ready to let "bygones be bygones." Or, is this a very clever trick on the part of Esau? In any case, Esau has a number of questions: "who are these?" and "what do these gifts mean?" Jacob uses this to testify about *favor* and *grace*. The family is God's gracious gift, His favor, to Jacob, and the gifts that Jacob has so generously sent ahead to Esau (see Gen. 32:13ff.) were to win Esau's favor. Jacob has received blessings, and he passes on a generous portion to sweeten the mood of his brother, if he needed that.

Jacob insists on giving Esau a gift (33:8–11)

It may be that Jacob feels some guilt in taking the blessing away by deception in Genesis 27. God has showered him with abundance, and he shares some of it Esau. The word sometimes translated as gift is literally "blessing" in verse 11. Jacob had obtained the blessing pronouncement from his father by means of deception in Genesis 27. Now he is ready to give Esau a generous portion of blessing in the form of these many valuable gifts. Perhaps it is Jacob's way of making amends.

But Esau tries to dissuade him. He claims that he has been blessed; he has plenty (v. 9). What is the source of these blessings? We are not told. If Jacob is somewhat thrown off balance, we readers almost certainly are. What has happened in Esau's heart? There have been tears from both of these elderly men. Either Esau is a great actor, or he is much different from the person we saw at the end of Genesis 27, when he was fully determined to kill Jacob.

The Life of Jacob

A further irony is Jacob's remark about Esau and the "face of God." See Genesis 32:24–32, where Jacob had seen the face of God in the person of the mysterious Stranger with whom he had wrestled through the night. As a divine Person, He could have destroyed Jacob, but He does not. Now in Genesis 33, Jacob meets a powerful brother, one whose 400 men could have destroyed him. But Esau does not do so. Jacob is experiencing the protecting power of God. Earlier as well, it was God who intervened by means of a dream to tell Laban to leave Jacob alone, and Laban did not attack Jacob. Laban barked loudly, but there was no bite. But we do not read that Esau has received any night vision or dream to tell him to deal kindly with his brother. Yet clearly Esau has changed. God's Spirit blows where He wills.

Jacob insists on going in separate ways (33:12–16)

Esau wants his forces to go with Jacob and his household, perhaps as a kind of armed force to escort his brother, his family, and his belongings into Canaan. Jacob declines this offer, giving the excuse that the children and the female animals are too weak to make this trip at a vigorous speed. We find this excuse of Jacob not convincing, seeing that Jacob and his retinue had traveled away from Laban in very good time. It may very well be that Jacob is suspicious about his brother's motive in making this offer: can Jacob fully trust Esau? Jacob tells Esau that he can just travel on ahead. Eventually Jacob and his household will arrive in Mt. Seir. (This is the region south of the Dead Sea where the Edomites, the descendants of Esau, will live). But Jacob apparently never goes there. Has he deceived his brother one more time? Does Jacob simply become "too busy" with living in the Succoth region that he just never gets around to traveling down south to Mt. Seir?

Esau and Jacob will separate as brothers again, if not

Jacob and Esau Meet Again as Brothers

actually friends. No boundary stones are needed to mark a border, a kind of "fence," between them (as in the case of Laban and Jacob; Gen. 31:51–54). Will this good will between the twin brothers last during their lifetime? How will their descendants relate to each other? Time will tell, but that story will not be as pleasant as the story told here in Genesis 33.

Jacob begins to move in (33:17–20)

Esau travels to the Seir region, while Jacob settles at Succoth (which means "booths, tabernacles"). The text tells us that he has safely come back home. He eventually comes to live at Shechem in the central part of Canaan. It is here that "Jacob's Well" would be dug (cf. John 4:5–6). Jacob is coming home, as he is settling in with his household. Remember that this is the land God has promised to him and his forefathers! See how this is an answer to his prayer in Genesis 28:21. Later he moves on to the Shechem region (about 30 miles or 48 km distance).

This is the Promised Land, to be sure, and yet Jacob must purchase land from the Shechemites. But see what he does with it: he sets up an altar. The significance is that this spot of worship serves as a kind of outpost for the kingdom of God. In the midst of Canaanite idolatry and paganism, here is a place where the true God might be worshiped and honored. The NIV tells us that Jacob calls it "El Elohe Israel," i.e., God, the God of Israel.

What does this say about Jacob, with regard to his attitude toward God and his attitude toward his own new name? Perhaps it tells us that God's Spirit is further sanctifying the heart and life of Jacob. This is wonderful to see in other people in God's great story: they never stand still, so to speak, but God moves them from one glory to another glory as they undergo many experiences in their lives. Their faith deepens, their hope becomes more secure, and their love matures. Biblical saints still have many flaws, and the devil keeps seeking to trip them up, but God begins a good work in Abram, in Isaac, in Jacob, in David, and in many more, and He will bring that good work to completion (cf. Phil. 1:6).

Lesson 12: Points to ponder and discuss

1. Jacob arranges matters to gain Esau's favor and also to place his most loved family members (Rachel and Joseph) in the better defensive position. Is this cowardice on Jacob's part, or is it wisdom and simply being shrewd?
2. Read Genesis 27:26 and 29. What is the irony of this kiss in the light of earlier events? Why does Jacob bow seven times? Is this a kind of "overkill" on Jacob's part, too much humbling of himself?
3. What accounts for Esau's change of heart toward Jacob? Is it his "own good nature" that "acts as a check on him," as one commentator puts it (cf. Hamilton, *Genesis 18–50*, p. 345)? Or, do God the Father and His Spirit have a very important role to play here? Apart from regeneration, what is the heart attitude of human being toward God and the neighbor? See Heidelberg Catechism, Q/A Lord's Day 3.
4. Why was Jacob so fearful of Esau? What things had God said and done earlier that should have removed Jacob's fears? There are many places in the Bible where we read, "Don't be afraid!" And yet God's children are so often afraid. Why is this so? What is it that can drive away our fears?

Jacob and Esau Meet Again as Brothers

5. What was the purpose of the many gifts that Jacob presses upon Esau? What is the purpose of gift-giving, whether in ancient times or in our times? How often do we give in order to get? Can gift-giving become a subtle form of manipulation? How is God's giving so different from our practices?
6. By changing Esau, what has God brought about that will advance His kingdom through Jacob? Or, to put it in a different way, what would have happened if Esau had come out to annihilate Jacob and his family? What does all this say about our God and the outworking of His saving plan?
7. Jacob sets up an altar for the true worship of God, even in pagan Canaan. Christian congregations also form as worshiping centers in the midst of a wicked culture. How can the presence of a church (even the church's name!) serve as a light, a grace-bearing outpost, in your community?

Lesson 13

Jacob's Sons Dishonor the Covenant Sign

Read Genesis 34

Introduction

When Genesis 33 ended, everything seemed to be going Jacob's way. Jacob and his household have arrived at Shechem, a significant city in central Canaan. They are camped within sight of the city itself. There is now peace, perhaps even good feelings, between Jacob and his twin brother Esau. Jacob has bought land and set up an altar to worship the true God, the God who has kept His word to Jacob and brought him back to the Promised Land. All appears well. But Genesis 33 also ended with the mention of the names of Hamor and his son Shechem, the local Canaanites who become very important in Genesis 34. The text is setting us up by means of these names for further developments in this chapter.

Where is God again?

The reader will note that God is mentioned in Genesis 33:20 ("El Elohe Israel" means "El, the God of Israel"). God again speaks to Jacob in Genesis 35:1. But the name of God is not mentioned at all in Genesis 34. To be sure, God is never absent from His people, yet it is as if God steps off the page for a moment in order to distance Himself, as it were, from the actions of Jacob's family in Genesis 34. When you read the Bible, always take note where God is, what He does, and what He says. God is textually "absent" in Genesis 34. So why is this chapter in the Bible? What is God revealing to His church here?

The Life of Jacob

Dinah defiled by a Canaanite (34:1-4)

This is the only story about Dinah in the Bible, but throughout the entire chapter, we never hear her speak! Her words are not recorded for us. There are perhaps five or six conversation scenes in Genesis 34, but Dinah does not join in the conversation. At least the text does not record her words, if she does speak. She is a daughter who is "seen but not heard," and even then, she is barely seen.

Dinah was the only named daughter of Jacob and Leah, born after Leah had given birth to six sons for Jacob (see Gen. 30:21). It is likely that the events of Genesis 30-33 would have taken at least eight years, and thus Dinah's age is thought to be about 15 or 16 years old. With so many brothers in the family of Jacob, is it possible that Dinah was simply seeking other women friends in the area? If so, was this so wrong?

Whatever Dinah's motivations were, her exposure to the women of Shechem also allows her to catch the eye of the young man Shechem, the son of Hamor, the local ruler. Verse 2 identifies him as a "Hivite," one of the people who were settled in Canaan at this time. Thus Dinah is seeking association, even friendship, with the people of the land who do not worship the true God, people who were pagans. Dinah's desire for a wider circle of friends will not end well, as the text tells us in verse 2. Listen to this unhappy escalation: "saw her . . . took her . . . violated her."

What happens here reminds us of a later incident in the household of King David (II Sam. 13), where his son Amnon rapes his half-sister Tamar. After that assault, Amnon despised Tamar. Not so in Genesis 34. In fact, Shechem loves Dinah and speaks tenderly to her (v. 3). He wants to marry the girl he has violated.

At this point a question arises about what actually happened with Dinah, and the commentators are not agreed. Was it rape, a crime of violence? The English verb

Jacob's Sons Dishonor the Covenant Sign

"violated" (v. 2) suggests violence, but the word in the original does not necessarily mean that. It can mean humiliate or even suppress, an action that can occur without violence. We do not read that Dinah resisted Shechem, as David's daughter Tamar did with Amnon in II Samuel 13. Shechem appears to love Dinah, and he wants to marry her, something a rapist does not desire with his victim. Perhaps what he did to Dinah falls along the lines of what Biblical law would later condemn as fornication or seduction, intimacy outside of marriage. Genesis 2 is clear as to the norms of marriage: one man and one woman are joined in a lifelong bond of union, a union that is sealed with vows that are taken *before* there is physical intimacy, which is part of the "one flesh" aspect of marriage.

We should be careful to point out that we do not "blame the victim" (Dinah), that is, if she was unwilling to be intimate with Shechem. We read in verse 26 that she is taken from Shechem's house, and we are hard pressed to say that she was being held there against her will. Nor do we read that she is unwilling to marry Shechem. Still, the text is clear that it is Shechem who "violated" her, and that is something that should never happen in Israel, among God's covenant people. This sin will now set in motion the events of retaliation.

The families respond to the crisis (34:5-7)

Shechem goes to his father to tell him to "get this girl" to be his wife. Shechem now falls back on traditional customs as he wants his father to arrange the marriage. Quite obviously the modern practice of "dating" was not an option for Shechem! And father Hamor goes to Jacob in order to enter into the negotiations that would lead to marriage (or so Shechem hopes). Jacob's response, on the other hand, is silence: he cannot respond alone as long as his sons are away with the family's livestock. When they learn of what happened to Dinah, they are furious.

The Life of Jacob

The Canaanite appeal (34:8–12)

The desire of Hamor and his son Shechem is revealed in verses 8–10 (and later in verses 21–23). The first speech is an attractive offer for Jacob and his entire family to live with these Canaanites, to intermarry with them, and to trade with them. In other words, just "blend in with us," say these Canaanite leaders. "We don't need to be separate from each other." Hamor and Shechem appear ready to give these aliens (Jacob's family) citizenship in this land. But this offer is really "forbidden fruit": it appears good, even attractive, but in the end it will bring death. Temptations are never presented to look ugly or unattractive. Otherwise they would not tempt us! Also, we never hear any confession of sin or any apologies from the Canaanites. Just ignore the sin that was committed: it is time to "move on." But the sin will keep festering.

The Israelite counteroffer (34:13–17)

While Hamor and Shechem offer glowing terms of inclusion, Jacob's sons plan deceit as Jacob seems to go into the background. But this deception reminds us of Jacob's own deceit earlier with his father Isaac. "False face hides what false heart does know." Intermarrying with people who are not circumcised is disgraceful, they tell these Canaanites. Dinah will be given in marriage if, and only if, all the males of Shechem submit to circumcision. This is the deal-breaker: if the Shechemite men do this, then they all can become *one people* (v. 16).

Genesis 17 reveals that the LORD had imposed circumcision upon believing Abraham and his entire household as a sign of the covenant between God and His people. In the physical organ of generation every male member of the covenant would bear throughout his life a reminder that he had been set apart by God's gracious decision, representative that only God can cut away the sin

Jacob's Sons Dishonor the Covenant Sign

in our lives and that we are called by God to a new obedience. Therefore, circumcision was an outward act, one that was representative of an inner reality. But that inward reality can only be worked by the operation of the Holy Spirit. In God's covenant family every male was to be circumcised on the eighth day of his life: having lived through one week (7 days) of the old creation, he began a new week on the eighth day as a marked man in his flesh. Imposed upon such a covenant community was the calling to a new way of life. Circumcision was thus an Old Testament sacrament of the covenant of grace, with the meaning given by God's Word.

How tragic and how sad it is to read this story in Genesis 34, where Jacob's sons talk to the Shechemites about the physical sign, but we read nothing about God's covenant. We hear nothing about the gracious acts of the true and living God. The members of God's covenant—Dinah's brothers—are silent when it comes to submitting to the LORD. Instead, the sign of God's gracious favor becomes, in their angry and enraged hearts, a tactic in a strategy, a plot devised to massacre their neighbors. One man violated Dinah; Jacob's sons plot to wipe out every one of the males of Shechem. The covenant sign becomes the device of deception.

Persuading the Shechemites (34:18–24)

Amazingly, Shechem enthusiastically agrees! He wants to marry Dinah (v. 19: he is "delighted" with her). But father Hamor and honored son Shechem must now persuade the males of the town to submit to the knives of circumcision. This better be a very persuasive speech! And it is. But the angle of persuasion in this speech (vs. 21–24) is slightly different from that used with Jacob and his sons. The Shechemites are told that they should agree to this proposal in order to get the Israelites to live and trade

The Life of Jacob

among them. The clincher comes in verse 23: "Won't their livestock, their property and all their other animals become ours?" This is a shameless appeal to greed. "No pain, no gain" convinces the men that, in the end, the people of Shechem will come out ahead financially. The Israelites will blend in and then melt away.

Massacre and plundering (34:25-29)

The strategy is carried out by Dinah's full brothers, Simeon and Levi. By the third day after the circumcision, the fighting men of the city would have been temporarily weakened by fever, pain, and discomfort. Now two brothers strike (with support from their servants?). All the males of the city of Shechem are killed. Simeon and Levi are then joined by the rest of the brothers in carrying off the plunder of the city: all the animals, all the wealth, and the woman and children, presumably to be kept or sold as slaves. Deception and then horrific violence are perpetrated by Jacob's sons, by church members, sons who had the sign of the covenant in their own flesh. Where did these young(er) men learn such violence? How could they carry out such an atrocity? Does such evil lurk just below the surface in any of us or in all of us? God sanctifies, it's true, but so often it is "one step forward, then two steps back."

Now what? (34:30-31)

The chapter ends on a very sad note. Jacob finally speaks, but his speech lacks resolution and focus. "I'm afraid that you've ruined our reputation around here. Your violence puts us all in physical danger." The sons respond with a moral argument: "We acted to maintain justice with regard to our sister." The sad truth is this: whenever God's people act in disobedience, they place themselves outside of covenant protection. Furthermore, when we take the law into our own hands, our actions can be reckless,

Jacob's Sons Dishonor the Covenant Sign

destructive, and such brings dishonor on God's Name. To make things "right," did every male in Shechem need to die?

Lesson 13: Points to ponder and discuss

1. In Genesis 33 the redemptive story for Jacob and his family seems so positive after the good meeting with Esau. But then a crisis strikes the family in Genesis 34. While no one wants a crisis, much less real tragedy, what can Christians do to prepare themselves for a crisis or a tragedy? What are possible benefits to a crisis or tragedy that Christians can see only later on?
2. Where Jacob settles in this land is filled with spiritual risks, even physical risks. What things must Christian families consider when moving and settling elsewhere? Certainly one looks at the presence of Christian churches, Christian education, as well as physical safety. What other things must be considered? Should Christians forsake a lucrative job opportunity if such a move would harm a family spiritually?
3. Read Deuteronomy 7:1–6. How can this be applied to Christians today?
4. Perhaps Dinah was seeking friendship. Friendship is important, but our circle of friends can influence our lives, for good or ill. What kinds of friends did you have growing up, especially in high school and into adulthood? Are some of them still your friends? How do you—how can you—influence the kind of friends your own children have?

The Life of Jacob

5. Jacob's sons abuse the covenant sign of circumcision. Circumcision has passed away with the coming of Christ. Yet in the church today, what are possible ways that the things of the Christian faith and of the Christian church might be abused for one's own advantage?
6. Christians are the "salt of the earth" and "the light of the world." We are "in the world," but we are "not of the world." How can we do this? What can you and your family do to stay spiritually strong in Christ, and at the same time be a strong witness to the people around you?
7. What can possibly explain the frightful escalation of sin in Genesis 34: a daughter/sister violated initially, ending with the massacre of an entire city? Remember: these are the covenant sons of the patriarch Jacob, the "leader" of the Old Testament church at this time. Read about the people and events of Genesis 4 as you consider this question.

Lesson 14

At Bethel God Reaffirms His Covenant (Again!)

Read Genesis 35

Introduction

The sordid story of Genesis 34 reveals several things. The depravity of human nature is put on display, even coming to expression in the lives of God's covenant people. There is also the constant lure of temptation that comes to God's people to blend into the surrounding culture and thus lose their distinctive nature and calling as those who are identified as salt and light. But the chapter also shows us how God could be at work for the good of His people: the shocking massacre of the men of Shechem now puts a fear into Jacob that causes him to want to move on and move away from his settlement by Shechem.

Time to move (35:1)

It is God who calls Jacob back to Bethel. Jacob may want to move on, but it is God who puts the matter clearly before him. God sends Jacob back to a very significant spot: Bethel, where God had appeared to him. Covenant history occurred there, and Jacob must remember that, now with his whole family.

In this chapter we come full circle. God commands Jacob to return to Bethel with his family, and in this way, God moves His covenant family away from the area that had become dangerous due to the events of Genesis 34. Bethel God had appeared to Jacob in a dream when he was fleeing from his brother in Genesis 28. He will appear to him again (vs. 9–13).

The Life of Jacob

Jacob prepares his household (35:2-5)

Jacob must first prepare his family to meet with God. If Jacob appeared somewhat passive in Genesis 34, here he takes the leadership with his household. This includes the removal of all the "foreign gods" from their midst. Earlier we had read of Rachel taking her father's teraphim and then hiding them in her saddlebag (Gen. 31:19). But apparently she was not alone in having superstitious beliefs and pagan charms with her: other family members and household servants have them as well! Jacob calls them "foreign" gods. What does this mean? These are not the gods that have revealed anything to their forefathers. False gods have nothing to say. It is the living God who called Abram out of Ur of the Chaldees, and it is the living God who reaffirmed His covenant promises again and again to Jacob's grandfather and father. All other gods are "foreign," that is, they come from somewhere else. They are, in fact, no gods at all!

Jacob requires his household to change the clothing they were wearing and to surrender even their earrings. These get buried under a particular oak tree. Read Deuteronomy 7:5 and 7:25. Idols of foreign gods were to be smashed and, if possible, burned in fire. Physical remains must be removed lest our hearts—which can be "factories" that manufacture idols—be led astray.

We will see a similar kind of preparation when Israel comes to meet the LORD at Mt. Sinai (cf. Exod. 19:10, 14). They must purify themselves and bathe to be ceremonial clean, for God is holy, a consuming fire, and He cannot even look upon sin. This is still true today. Thus we absolutely need a pure and spotless Mediator to present us before this holy God. We need the sinless Lamb of God, Jesus Christ.

The terror of God subdues the surrounding people as Jacob's family makes its way to Bethel. This is an important

At Bethel God Reaffirms His Covenant (Again!)

point: it is not the case that the Canaanites are afraid, first of all, of Jacob's fierce sons. The fear in their hearts comes from the Lord God. Later on, God will do a similar thing with Israel's enemies as they go to the Promised Land (cf. Exod. 23:27). Rahab will tell the two spies that fear had fallen upon the people of Jericho: their hearts "melted" (Josh. 2:9, 11, 24).

Jacob builds an altar at Bethel (35:6–7)

Genesis records several times and places where altars were built (see Gen. 12:7; 13:4, 18). God's people recognized that they needed to come before the living and holy God to worship Him. Likely they would come with an appropriate gift, bringing a sacrifice in the form of a perfect animal as their substitute, one that would die in their place.
This would all become formalized in the Mosaic covenant. Yet the realities of the gospel work of Jesus Christ and His message for sinners were already in place in the Old Testament period, even if these truths were not yet worked out as they would be in the more sophisticated practices described in the Mosaic covenant (e.g., Leviticus 1–7). Bethel is "God's house," since the true God had made Himself known at this place. Jacob's altar is a physical signpost of the presence of God in His people and in His world.

God repeats redemptive promises—again! (35:9–13)

Truly we have come full circle! God appears, i.e., some kind of visible presence occurs that Jacob could see. He had seen God in a dream, and at Peniel he had wrestled with God. Furthermore, God's words here recall His covenantal promises made in Genesis 17, 22, and 28:13ff.
He pronounces a blessing with the focus upon *children* and *land*. These have been a major thread that has run through the stories of Abraham, Isaac, and now Jacob. Children

The Life of Jacob

(seed) and land have been the two "pillar promises" of the covenant of grace in the narratives of the patriarchs. Those children today include God's people in the whole world, and that land of Canaan was only an anticipation for all the earth that God now claims for His Son, the Lord Jesus Christ. Children and land, as well as blessing and protection, are the key promises that God not only makes, but He also fulfills through Jesus Christ and by the work of Jesus Christ.

God also confirms the name change that He made when Jacob had wrestled with the mysterious, divine Stranger at Peniel. Jacob has become *Israel* (meaning "God struggles," or, "he struggles with God"). Over all these years, God has built up the man Jacob and His covenant people. God shows Himself to be gracious and incredibly patient with a man whose life has been somewhat spotty and unattractive to any observer. God has wrestled with this man (even physically!), and He is not finished with Jacob or with his family. He is longsuffering with the people of His church because we, God's children, so often fall so far short of God's glory. This is going to be a history-long wrestling match. Yet by grace, God's people will win since Jesus Christ has already won the victory for them on Calvary's cross and on Easter morning.

Jacob responds to God's words (35:14–15)

Jacob, in turn, answers God's appearance here in much the same manner as he had responded in Genesis 28, over 20 years earlier. He sets up a stone pillar and anoints it with a drink offering and oil. This consecration is one way to mark out a kind of "signpost" for God's Kingdom in this world. Canaan does not belong to the wicked Canaanites, though they live there for the moment; it really belongs to God and the people that He allows to live with Him. It is, after all, the Promised Land, territory that God

At Bethel God Reaffirms His Covenant (Again!)

owns and He graciously chooses to give to His people.

The same is true today: this world is turned against the true God, even though He remains in sovereign control. In fact, Jesus Christ has been given all authority in heaven and earth, according to Matthew 28:18ff. Christians also set up signposts that point the way to a new reality! Therefore, Christians want schools to be genuinely Christian and businesses to operate according to biblical principles. We work for genuine justice in public affairs, and we seek peace and reconciliation in our society. The world must see the "signposts" of the coming Kingdom of God.

In the end at least two names are locked in place: Jacob is "Israel," the father of the people with that name. Plus, Luz has been re-identified as Bethel, "the house of God," one of many places where the living God came to His people to repeat the promise of the holy gospel for people who needed to hear it again.

Moving on

Genesis 35 records some further travels of this covenant household. They move on from Bethel to Ephrath (v. 16). Then Israel (note the use of this name!) moves again toward Migdal Eder (v. 21). He will also come to Hebron (the older name being Kiriath-arba) around the time when his father Isaac passes away.

Obituary notices

This chapter records the death of several people:

1. Deborah, Rebekah's nurse dies, and she is buried under the oak below Bethel. It is not exactly clear why we are told this. Has Rebekah died already? Did this (presumably elderly) nurse come to live with Jacob? We cannot be completely certain.

2. Rachel dies while giving birth to her second son, Benjamin ("son of the right hand," or, "the south").

The Life of Jacob

There is some irony in her death. She at one time said to Jacob, "Give me children, or I die!" When Joseph was born, she had hoped for another son. So now, when her second son is born, she dies in childbirth. But Rachel dies near Ephrath, i.e., Bethlehem (Ruth 1:2; Mic. 5:2), the village where our Lord Jesus Christ would be born, the One who would conquer death once and for all. Benjamin is the only son born in the Promised Land; the others all born in Paddan-Aram (Mesopotamia).

3. Isaac dies. We might say, "finally dies," since when he sensed his death approaching back in Genesis 27, that was at least two decades earlier. Reports of his imminent demise were greatly exaggerated! He had remained living in the southern region of the Promised Land. His age at death (180 years) was actually five years longer than his own father Abraham's age at death. There is a beautiful statement in verse 29, not to be missed, when we read that both twin sons, Esau and Jacob, join together to bury their aged father. Peace between the brothers seems to be holding.

These are all deaths in the Promised Land. Isaac is gathered to his family. Believers have the confidence that while we live, our life is defined by Christ, for Christ. Dying is never loss for the believer; it is gain (Phil. 1:21). God is the "God of Abraham, of Isaac, and of Jacob." See Matthew 22:29–32 (paralleled in Mark 12:26, 27 and Luke 20:37, 38). Though now they are physically dead, to our living God, they are alive.

At Bethel God Reaffirms His Covenant (Again!)

Lesson 14: Points to ponder and discuss
1. At the end of Genesis 34, Jacob was concerned about his reputation becoming a stench to his neighbors, and he feared for his safety and that of his family. What does our society today think of the Christian church and of Christian people? What testimony do our words and lives give to the world around us? Should we even care what opinion the world has of Christianity?
2. The "foreign gods," superstitious charms, etc., had to be removed, even buried, before Jacob's household could meet the LORD. Today published horoscopes are still with us, psychic readers do business in our cities, and witchcraft is still practiced in North America. Does this affect Christians you know? What explains this, especially in areas that supposedly have had a Christian heritage?
3. At Bethel, God repeated His gospel promises of children and land to Jacob. Why did Jacob need to hear this again? How many times did he hear it during his life? Why do Christian churches need to preach the gospel, and why do Christians need to hear it again? Can church members ever become tired of hearing that "old, old story"? If they do, why is that the case?
4. Rachel dies as she gives birth to her second son. She gives him the name Ben-Oni, "son of trouble," but Jacob overrules this by calling him Benjamin, "son of the right hand (or, the south)." Why, do you think, did Jacob give him such a name? Could it be, as some commentators suggest, that Jacob did not want the son of his beloved wife Rachel to go through life with a sad and negative name? How does Jacob treat Benjamin later when his ten sons want to take him to Egypt (when Joseph is in charge in Egypt)?

The Life of Jacob

5. Genesis 35:22 records that Reuben slept with Bilhah, who had been Rachel's maidservant. More importantly, she had become one of Jacob's concubines, the mother of Dan and Naphtali. How do the brothers react to this sexual sin? How does Israel respond to this? Compare their response to Dinah's violation in Genesis 34. To sleep with a man's concubines suggests that he wants to take over the reins of power and leadership. Read II Samuel 3:7; 16:20–22; and I Kings 2:22. Does Reuben want to usurp the leadership from his aged father? What does this act cost Reuben in the end (see Gen. 49:3, 4)?

6. It was Isaac's sense of his impending death that led to Jacob's deception and then Esau's hatred in Genesis 27. Isaac's actual death brings the brothers together in one last labor of love in which they together bury their father. What hope could Esau and Jacob have concerning life after death? What could other Old Testament saints have with respect to this? See Job 19:25–27; Psalm 17:15; 49:15.

Lesson 15

The History of the Older Brother, Esau

Read Genesis 36–37:1

Introduction

Genesis 35 completes the circle of Jacob's life that began with his flight to Paddan-Aram away from his brother Esau (Gen. 28:1–9). Genesis 35 in many ways summarizes the key elements in Jacob's life, especially those things that God had introduced into his life. Genesis 35 closes with two things that prepare us for the next portion of Genesis. First, we read a list of Jacob's children, grouped according to their mothers (Leah, Rachel, Bilhah, and Zilpah). Second, we also read that Esau and Jacob together bury their aged father Isaac. The venom of ill-will between the brothers at the time Jacob deceived his father in Genesis 27 is gone. That prepares us to read more of what became of Esau.

Surprise! here's the family of . . . Esau

Actually, we may be somewhat surprised by the inclusion of such a long chapter devoted exclusively to Esau, his family, and the nation that came from him. After all, didn't God say that the "older (Esau) shall serve the younger (Jacob)"? And we know from Malachi 1:2–3 that God loved Jacob, but He hated Esau. So there must be a good reason for God to include this family history of Esau for us to read.

Genesis 36 is frequently skipped over in most Bible reading and in many Bible studies. "What, another genealogy? All those difficult to pronounce names!" You can almost

The Life of Jacob

here it from family members at Bible reading time. Indeed, in the Old Testament at different points we meet a list of names of fathers, their children, and their grandchildren, and we may well wonder why. What does God want the community of faith to see and hear in these names? "All Scripture is breathed out by God," writes Paul to Timothy (II Tim. 3:16), and that would include the genealogies of the Old Testament.

Genesis 36:1 and 36:9 both include that phrase used in Genesis that periodically begins a new focus of interest. "These are the generations of . . ." or "This is the family history/record of . . ." the translations say. See Genesis 2:4; 5:1; 6:9, etc., for instances of this phrase. We may think it rather odd that Esau and his family line get an entire chapter in Genesis . . . and one of the longest in the entire book, at that! Let's consider what God is saying to us readers.

Two seeds in the story line

Abraham had two sons: Ishmael, the son of Hagar (the Egyptian maidservant), and Isaac, the son of Sarah (the free woman). Abraham's death and burial are recorded in Genesis 25:7–11. Right after that comes an account of Ishmael's family descendants. Although Ishmael is not the promised seed, God still says to Abraham that Ishmael would become a nation "because he is your offspring" (Gen. 21:13). God keeps His promises! So the text records—albeit briefly—Ishmael's family. It is like taking a brief turn off the main road to take note of a point of interest, and then we readers return to the main storyline. Once the text has glanced at Ishmael, it then throws the spotlight on the more important person at that point, namely, Isaac.

Something similar happens here in Genesis 36. Isaac has two sons: Esau, the physical firstborn, but the one whom

The History of the Older Brother, Esau

God does not choose, and then Jacob, the younger son, the one whom God chooses before he is even born. God tells us about Isaac and Jacob, but before He tells us of what happened in Jacob's family, He first directs our attention to Esau. He tells us that Esau also fathered a nation, a people, and that he was very wealthy as well. Once we note that, then the story of redemptive-history gets back on the main route again to focus on the covenant people, the family of Jacob.

Beyond that, we are reminded that there are two seeds that are traced in history: even in a covenant home there is one son of God's electing promise and another son who is not the promised seed. This does not mean that the son who is not the promised seed is automatically on his way to hell. The question of personal faith is a different question. In fact, one gets a different impression of who Esau (Edom) is when we read the text closely. Earlier we have read that Esau was very welcoming to Jacob, while Jacob was very afraid of his brother. Jacob had tried to soften the soul of his brother with wave after wave of gifts, but Esau says that this was not necessary. God has blessed him with wealth; Jacob could keep it all (see Gen. 33:9). Esau actually invited Jacob to settle together with him in the Mt. Seir region, but Jacob refuses. And the brothers bury their father together.

In the end it is clear that Esau is more than willing to "bury the hatchet"—and not in his brother's head! In the end Esau is warm to his brother, and we should not miss that point. They do not die as mutual enemies.

Esau is Edom

Would such brotherly affection had remained in their children! Several times in Genesis 36 (vs. 1, 8, 9, 43, etc.) we read that "Esau is Edom," and in this way the Bible is telling us about the future. From one man, Esau, came the nation of Edom (which means "red"). The names of his

The Life of Jacob

wives as given here differ from the names given in Genesis 26:14 and 28:9. Solutions to this question are not easy. Either Esau had more than three wives, or the names are altered in the text, or there may be another solution.

Amalek and Edom in the Exodus

In any case, Esau has three wives and five sons listed in Genesis 36, along with their descendants. We cannot comment on every name, but we draw attention to just this one person, Amalek. Genesis 36:12 tells us that Esau's son Eliphaz had a son with his concubine. This son, Amalek, became the father of the nation that attacked Israel after she was freed from slavery in Egypt. Exodus 17:8–13 records the first test that Israel had as a nation after the liberation. Joshua overcomes this enemy, but Amalek becomes the nation that is the paradigm of hostility against God's people. The LORD is at war with Amalek forever. Israel must never forget this (see Num. 24:20; Deut. 25:17–19)!

Later on, as the Israelites are getting closer to the Promised Land, they must skirt the land of Edom because the Edomites refused any brotherly kindness to God's people (see Num. 20:14–21). Even Israel's offer to pay for any water drunk by the animals receives a cold rebuff. "You may not pass through!" Edom says. National hostility has replaced brotherly hospitality.

Psalm 137 and Obadiah

Much later, while they are in exile in Babylon, the forlorn believers are homesick for Zion, the city of God. Part of this psalm from Babylon turns our attention to the Edomites. Psalm 137:7 reveals that the Edomites cheered the Babylonians on in destroying Jerusalem. "Tear it down!" they cried. In other words, "Destroy the city! Crush the church!" Even though Judah, the covenant people, was worthy of severe discipline, the attitude of

The History of the Older Brother, Esau

Edom was a perverse glee to see Zion destroyed. When did you last hear a sermon from Obadiah? The shortest book of the Old Testament is focused on the day of the Lord coming against Edom, while the Kingdom of God would triumph. This is good news!

Hope for Edom in David's tent (Amos 9:11–15)

The last Edomite known in the Bible is wicked king Herod (sometimes called "the Great") in Matthew 2. This is the king in Jerusalem who wanted to kill Christ after the Magi from the east alert him to the fact that a new "king of the Jews" had been born. Actually Herod was half-Idumean, Idumea being the name of the nation in southern Palestine near where the Edomite kingdom had been. As a half-Idumean ruler, installed by the Romans and hated by his own people, king Herod was "great," not because he was so good, but because he was so evil. He murdered members of his own family, and he feared any rival to his throne. He embodied the spirit of the great serpent, Satan, who was poised throughout the Old Testament era to devour the Child that was to be born to the mother, the Old Testament church. Revelation 12 pictures this so clearly for us. The insanity of sin becomes painfully obvious to us when we read that Herod orders a massacre of all male children in the Bethlehem region, two years and younger, in the hope that a quick thrust of a soldier's sword might destroy this new "king of the Jews." The Devil strikes out against the Christ through the evil of Herod.

Herod reminds us in a very sobering way that throughout history there are two seeds existing, and there is enmity between them. They are in conflict with each other. Yet the most that the seed of the serpent can do is bruise the heel of the Seed of the woman. Satan cannot, he will not, win.

The Seed of the woman culminates in the Lord Jesus Christ (Gal. 3:16). And all who believe in Jesus Christ are

The Life of Jacob

children (seed) of Abraham, born again by the power of the Holy Spirit. Even Edom can find hope in Him. Amos 9:11–15 closes off a prophetic book that is nearly unrelenting in its condemnation of Israel's sins. But God's grace gets in the last good word. Amos says that a time will come when God will restore the fallen tent of David. The nations—even Edom!—will find shelter, home and security, in the restoration of the kingdom of David.

Now switch to the Jerusalem council in Acts 15. The council hears the wonderful news that Gentiles are coming to saving faith in Jesus Christ: this is what the prophets had earlier said! Christ has died and has been raised from dead. These saving events have changed everything for all the nations of the world. True, the two spiritual seeds still exist in the world, and they will exist in this world until the end of time. But the New Testament makes clear that we should never think in terms of the two seeds as a racial or national thing, but as a spiritual matter. God's electing grace and wondrous love reaches into all cultures, all tribes, all nations, and all peoples. Even people who are descended from Edom can be reached by the power of God's saving grace in Jesus Christ. God's grace is never chained, and it does not stop at political borders.

This is true today as well. There may be nations that are largely hostile now to the gospel of God, as Edom was hostile to Israel throughout history. Yet from those nations there will come an elect remnant, chosen to everlasting life in Jesus Christ and brought to saving faith by the Word of the Lord, in the power of the Holy Spirit.

The History of the Older Brother, Esau

Lesson 15: Points to ponder and discuss

1. In your Bible reading, have you ever skipped over the genealogies of Genesis 5, 10, and 11, or the long name lists in Ezra and I Chronicles (be honest now!)? Why or why not? If you have omitted them in your Bible reading and study, what were some of the reasons? Did you ever make a little extra effort to find out what the reason is for including them in the inspired Scriptures?
2. Esau and Jacob appear to be reconciled to each other in the closing years of their lives. The Edomites, Esau's children, become very hostile to the Israelites, Jacob's children. What might be the reasons to explain such hostility?
3. Edom rejoiced to see Jerusalem fall to the Babylonians. Do we see a similar kind of smug satisfaction on the part of non-believers when Christian churches as well as Christian leaders and people have shortcomings and sins, personal and public? Why is that so? What do we learn about human nature? What might God be teaching us in those times?
4. Christian missionaries have reached many nations and peoples in today's world. In some places such mission efforts may be only through radio broadcasting and literature distribution. In what nations today is there great hostility to Christianity, either on the part of the government and/or the society?
5. The "Voice of the Martyrs" is an organization that keeps track of the persecution of Christians in various parts of the world. What can Christians in North America do to assist such churches and these persecuted Christians? Prayers and letters? Political pressure? Physical and material assistance? How can your congregation become more aware of the suffering of fellow believers?

The Life of Jacob

6. Read Deuteronomy 23:7, 8. The Edomite is a brother, not to be abhorred, even though the Edomites remained hostile to God's people throughout history (see Amos 1:11–12). Is this an example of our LORD's teaching to "love your enemies"? If so, what does loving your enemies include?

Lesson 16

Israel and Sons Sojourn in Egypt

Read Genesis 36:2-11, 31-35

Introduction
The final section of the book of Genesis focuses on the story of the family of Jacob. What became of his children? This is the meaning of Genesis 37:2, where the last major section of Genesis is introduced. We notice again that though Jacob is mentioned in verse 2, the next chapters (Gen. 37–50) focus on Joseph, Judah, and the rest of the sons of Jacob. The inspired spotlight now falls more on the next generation of patriarchs. To be sure, Jacob is still in the story line, but he begins to recede to the background in these chapters.

Israel loves Joseph more (37:2–11)
The story line from Genesis 37 really now switches to Joseph (and Judah). Yet the Joseph story is all part of the account of Jacob (Gen. 37:2). God's work in Joseph's heart and life is *for His covenant people,* to save them all alive.
There are some striking parallels in the household of Jacob and that of his own father Isaac. Isaac had favored Esau while Rebekah had favored Jacob. Jacob had a favorite wife, the beautiful Rachel, and she born a son, Joseph, while the family was still in Paddan-Aram. He is a son of his father's old age, and Israel loves him more than his other sons. This favoritism does not escape notice by the other sons, Joseph's half-brothers. Jacob even favors Joseph with a special coat, perhaps one with long sleeves, the kind

The Life of Jacob

worn by royal children. Later on, King David's daughter Tamar will wear a similar kind of garment (see II Sam. 13:18). Perhaps Israel (Jacob) is giving out a not so subtle hint that Joseph will be the son to inherit the leadership role in the family after Israel dies, even though he is not the oldest son. God speaks through Joseph's dreams, and the dreams are well understood by the members of the family. Joseph will rule. But even father Israel finds it strange that the second dream (the heavenly bodies bowing to Joseph) indicates that the father will also bow down to Joseph. Does the father bow to the son? In verse 10, father Israel asks Joseph, "Will your mother and I and your brothers actually come and bow down to the ground before you?" This gives Israel more to think about: what does this actually mean?

The story is well-known and often told. Joseph goes to check on his brothers, and they first imprison him in a well, and then they sell him to a traveling caravan of merchants who are headed for Egypt. They concoct a story of finding Joseph's special coat with blood on it. Here is another irony: just as Jacob used goat meat and goat skins to deceive his father Isaac in Genesis 27:5–13, so now Jacob's sons use goat blood to cause their father Jacob to think that a wild animal attacked and then ate his precious son Joseph.

Jacob had received the "news" of the death of Joseph particularly hard. He refused to allow his children to comfort him. His favorite wife Rachel was dead, and now his favorite son was also dead. In his old age, Jacob experiences tremendous personal pain and heartache. To lose a child, any child, is always a devastating event. But when it is the favorite son of your favorite wife, it was crushing to this poor old man. Jacob does not allow any words or actions of comfort to soften his grief (vs. 34–35).

Jacob sends his sons to Egypt (42:1–5, 29–38)

Jacob does not come back into the story until Genesis 42

Israel and Sons Sojourn in Egypt

when his family is becoming really hungry because of famine. Egypt had become the breadbasket for the world following the seven years of abundant harvests. But then famine strikes the Near East, and the land of Canaan is also affected. Jacob sends ten of his sons to buy grain in Egypt. He holds Benjamin back, because "harm might come to him" (Gen. 42:4). The text does not tell us this explicitly, but we readers may wonder if Jacob thinks that the harm may come from his ten sons! After all, Benjamin is the only son left of his beloved wife Rachel. He is willing to have his ten sons risk harm in Egypt, but he is still very protective of Benjamin.

At the end of the chapter Jacob comes back into the account when the brothers retell the story of what had happened in Egypt, especially the fact that the harsh ruler of Egypt demanded that the youngest son come the next time. Jacob's grief continues. "Everything is against me!" he cries out (verse 36).

Yet in fact things were not against him. This will become apparent later on, but, as they say, hindsight is always "20–20." The perspective of faith is described in Romans 8:28ff. Many things can be against the elect of God, but in Christ, we are "more than conquerors." Indeed nothing can separate us from the love of God which is ours in Christ Jesus our Lord!

Jacob, however, cannot see this at the end of Genesis 42. In his mind Benjamin is "the only one left" (v. 38). Jacob sees nothing but grief lining his final journey to death (Sheol).

Israel resends his sons to Egypt (43:1–14)

Desperate times call for desperate measures. The famine remains severe for people living in Canaan, including the members of the covenant household of Jacob. In this chapter he is called "Israel" (see Gen. 43:6, 8, 11; 45:28;

The Life of Jacob

46:1, 2, 5), but then at Genesis 45:25, 26, he is called "Jacob" again. Why is this done?

Israel (once called Jacob!) finally relents and gives permission to send young Benjamin along with the ten brothers to Egypt. How heavy his heart must have been to see him leave on this journey. Jacob is becoming resigned to losing his sons, one after the other: Joseph, then Simeon, and now beloved Benjamin.

Good news revives the heart of Jacob (45:25-28)

Jacob finds the news of Joseph being still alive to be unbelievable! How could something that had been so certain in his mind before—Joseph's death—now be turned around? The NIV says in Genesis 45:26 that he was stunned; literally, it says that his heart was numb, even "cold." He went into shock and denial. "Where did my sons get such a crazy, tall tale?" But when the words of his sons cannot convince him, the physical evidence of Egyptian carts eventually persuades him. Israel's years of mourning and grief give way to joy as he anticipates meeting his beloved son once more before he closes his own eyes in death. When he believes the good news, his heart lives again and is no longer numb or cold.

An 'immanuel' promise in the night (46:1-4)

Once again God, as it were, holds Jacob's hands and encourages him on the road to Egypt. God speaks His Word so that Israel/Jacob can live and act in peace. Take note of the several parts of God's word to Israel during that night vision. First, God identifies Himself as the God of his father (cf. Gen. 26:24). The same God is ours today, faithful in all generations of His people.

Second, God tells Israel not to be afraid. This same encouragement is often given in the Bible to people who are in a situation where fear is both understandable and

Israel and Sons Sojourn in Egypt

present. Israel is about to see his son, he believes, but he is also entering the mighty country of Egypt.

Third, God reminds Israel that he will make him into a great nation. Verses 8–27 tell us that his family is already becoming sizeable! But there is more to come. God will continue to enlarge the covenant family until the word "nation" becomes the more fitting word to describe it.

Fourth, God says—again!—that He will be with Israel. God will accompany Israel and his family as they journey down into Egypt, and He will be with Israel to bring him out again. "God with us" is the meaning of that wonderful name "Immanuel," one of the comforting names of our Redeemer, Jesus Christ (Matt. 1:22, 23). Matthew 28:20 tells that the Lord Jesus, risen from the dead and given universal authority, is with His church until the close of this age. What a comfort we have in the midst of our calling!

Jacob blesses Pharaoh (47:7–12)

Joseph makes the arrangements for his father and brothers to meet Pharaoh, the ruler of Egypt. Remarkably, this aged patriarch Jacob has an audience with Pharaoh. I call it remarkable because the Egyptians believed Pharaoh to be a living god. Twice we read that Jacob "blesses" the Pharaoh (Gen. 47:7, 10). The word we translate as "bless" can be understood as "greet," but this is still quite an event. Quite a change from the time when Jacob slept out in the open at Bethel with nothing more in his hand than his staff! Now his own son is in charge of the well-being of Egypt, and he meets, greets (blesses) Pharaoh! Later on, when the Israelites would leave Egypt and its slavery, the Pharaoh would send them away with the request, "And bless me also" (Exod. 12:32). Pharaoh would be beaten, and he would admit that Israel and Israel's God was greater than he.

The word of blessing is one of the themes that runs through the book of Genesis. In Genesis 1 God creates the

The Life of Jacob

sea creatures and mankind, and then He "blesses" them so that they might be fruitful and abundant. In Genesis 12:1–3 God called Abram from his own family in order to make him a great nation. Whoever blesses Abram and his family would receive blessing. Through Abram's family the nations of the world would be blessed.

Something of that is seen here. Because of Joseph, Egypt and many starving people receive blessing in the form of food, sustenance. Pharaoh recognizes this, and he in turn provides blessing to Jacob and his family in the form of the "best of the land," Goshen, where Jacob and his entire household could settle with their flocks and herds.

Yet the speech of Jacob strikes as somewhat negative. He tells the Pharaoh, "My years have been few and difficult" (v. 9). He enters Egypt at age 130, and he lives another 17 years there before he dies. To us, 130 years are not a few! But have the years of Jacob been difficult? To be sure, everyone's life has joys and sorrows, ups and downs. What have been Jacob's particular burdens, and have they outweighed in number and severity the times of joy and prosperity that he has enjoyed?

Israel in Egypt: it sounds ominous! And it would become a serious threat to the covenant family of God later on as the story in Exodus would tell it. But for the moment, God has brought Israel—the man Jacob and his children—to a kind of oasis on the road back to Paradise. They live in the best part of Egypt, but this is only a sojourn, for God's people do not have an abiding place in Egypt—or in this present world.

Israel and Sons Sojourn in Egypt

Lesson 16: Points to ponder and discuss
1. You may have heard the saying, "The apple does not fall far from the tree." In what ways do the sons of Jacob show something of the nature of their own father Jacob?
2. Trace the life of Jacob up to the point before the time he learns that Joseph is still alive. It has been a kind of roller-coaster of danger and blessing, times of fear and then faith. What have been the challenges to his faith that he has faced? In what ways has he grown in faith? In what areas of his life does he still need to grow? What difference has the grace of God made in his life?
3. Can you understand Jacob/Israel's reluctance to believe his sons with most of their stories and explanations of things? When a person stops telling the truth, he becomes suspect in all his words. What do we learn here regarding words and actions of truth and integrity?
4. Why does God appear to Israel at Beersheba in Genesis 46:2ff.? When Abram had gone to Egypt in Genesis 12:10ff. because of a famine, that was a problem because of Abram's deception. Later on in Genesis 26:1, 2, there was another famine, and the Lord had not allowed Isaac to go to Egypt. But now it appears that going to Egypt is okay with God. Why? What might account for the difference?
5. Why does the man Jacob become named "Israel" more and more in the story? Could the text be making a subtle and gradual transition to having us think about the *nation* of Israel? How is the man *Jacob* giving way to the nation *Israel* in the progress of redemptive-history?

The Life of Jacob

6. Settling in Goshen was a physical blessing. But is Goshen a good place to live, a fine choice for this large household? What positive qualities does it hold for Israel? What are the potential dangers for these people in Goshen and Egypt? What happens to church people when they lose their focus on their true and abiding home? How can "the best of this earth" become a snare to Christians?

Lesson 17

By Faith Jacob Blessed Joseph's Sons

Read Genesis 48

Introduction

Jacob and all his family have now moved into Goshen, the best part of Egypt. God clearly allowed this move during the days when Joseph was a powerful leader in Egypt, and the Pharaoh was kindly disposed toward Joseph's family. In the next several centuries the family of Jacob will grow into a mighty people, the nation of Israel, under the blessing of God (Gen. 47:27). But there would be no one "tribe of Joseph," but rather, from one man Joseph there would come two separate tribes as Jacob adopts Joseph's sons as equal to all of his other sons. At least questions come immediately to mind: 1) why does Jacob do this, and 2) why is so much Biblical text given over to recall this? What message is God giving to His people in Jacob's words and actions?

Jacob's speech to Joseph (48:1–7)

The chapter opens with an illness scene which is really a deathbed scene. We have been at a supposed "deathbed" before, namely, when Isaac earlier thinks that death is near (Gen. 27:1ff.). When Isaac believed that he was at death's doorstep, he wanted to pronounce his fatherly blessing as the patriarchal head of the family on his favorite son, Esau.

Joseph and his two oldest sons make their way over to his Jacob's residence. This gives Jacob an opportunity to put his remaining energy into a speech and a blessing ceremony,

The Life of Jacob

both of which are significant for the future of God's people. The things that Jacob says here will have impact down through the centuries as the nation of Israel develops and lives in the Promised Land of Canaan. Joseph and his sons must hear these words in order to understand what Jacob is about to do. But, even more importantly, we who read the story today might be able to trace how the hand of God leads His people in history and how He guides all things according to His great plan.

The first thing that Jacob recalls takes us back to his dream at Luz (renamed Bethel). When Jacob was fleeing from his brother, God appeared to him in a dream. Jacob calls God here, "God Almighty," i.e., "El Shaddai." Most likely this particular name for God identifies Him as a God who is strong and powerful (like the mountains), the God who can do whatever He wills to do, the God who is able to make everything in creation bend to His will and submit to His power. This was the divine name with which God identified Himself to Abraham in Genesis 17:1. In that context God spoke to Abraham about the great promise of descendants (seed) and land. Those things are the same items of interest in Genesis 28 at Luz (Bethel) in Jacob's dream! And that gracious promise is not yet fully realized in Genesis 48. Yet Jacob wants Joseph to know about God's revelation in a dream. After all, Joseph is not the only dreamer in redemptive-history! God spoke to many Old Testament saints by means of a dream or vision (cf. Heb. 1:1).

God's blessing would create a "community of peoples" from Jacob, and his descendants would receive the Promised Land as an "everlasting possession" (v. 4). That is the "old, old story" that God has put before the heart and mind of Abraham, Isaac, Jacob, and now Joseph and his sons. The essential message had never changed, but it got richer and fuller as time went on, even as the community of faith was growing in number and getting closer to the Promised Land.

By Faith Jacob Blessed Joseph's Sons

That story would reach one stage of fulfillment when the people of Israel come into the land of Canaan, but it would reach a higher level when Christ secures our entry into the new creation by His own work of salvation.

Jacob has given his son and grandsons a short history lesson. Once again we are impressed with how crucial history is in the Bible and in our faith. The center of this history lesson is God's great faithfulness: He did not give up on Jacob. Such mercy in a relationship is carried out through the work of the Holy Spirit. Our own sanctification and perseverance in the faith is based upon God's preservation. What a story to tell the next generations! What a legacy to leave behind as you realize that you are not going to stay in this world forever!

It is in that context that Jacob declares his intention to adopt Joseph's sons as his very own. Joseph took "Manasseh and Ephraim" (mentioned in verse 1 in the order of their birth) along with him. But as Jacob speaks, he says that he adopts "Ephraim and Manasseh" (the new order of importance) to be sons on an equal par with the other sons of Jacob. Thus, the favorite son (Joseph) of the favorite wife (Rachel) gets divided, so to speak, in order to become two tribes! Jacob recalls the sad loss of Rachel when she had died in Canaan and was then buried near Bethlehem. But looking ahead, he elevates these two sons of Joseph to patriarchal status. Obviously, Jacob had given this some thought ahead of time.

Joseph's sons presented to Israel (48:8–14)

Verse 10 probably explains why Jacob asks the question in verse 8, "Who are these?" His eyesight is poor. And the thoughtful reader remembers Genesis 27, when Isaac thinks he is about to die. So there are some parallels here.
But there are also differences: Jacob deceived Isaac earlier in order to obtain the fatherly blessing. Isaac unknowingly

pronounces the blessing on the younger son, although he thinks it is the older son, Esau. But in Genesis 48, although Jacob's eyesight has dimmed greatly, yet he knows what he is doing when he blesses the younger son. By asking "Who are these?" Jacob may be following good legal procedure to be certain that the proper parties are both present and identified. It is similar to when Isaac asks if it is indeed Esau who is present with him (see Gen. 27:18, 24, 32).

In his answer, Joseph identifies the boys standing with him as gifts from God. So it is! Joseph had married a daughter of an Egyptian priest. Joseph and his wife Asenath had at least two boys: Manasseh (from "to forget"?) and Ephraim ("twice fruitful"), as recorded in Genesis 41:50–52. Children are God's gifts in order to carry on the faith once for all delivered to the saints and to carry on the divine project of filling this world with people who serve the true God aright.

To have these two young boys before him, must have given Jacob deep joy and satisfaction. He has been moved from once thinking that Joseph was dead, to now being able to bless Joseph's sons. Who would have thought this possible?

Joseph had presented his sons according to the normal procedure so that the younger son would be on Jacob's left side while the older boy (Manasseh) would be on Jacob's right side, the side of the favored one. Joseph thinks, "My older son Manasseh gets the main blessing."

Jacob blesses Joseph (48:15–16)

In blessing Joseph, Jacob has in mind both of his sons, as he says in verse 16. In reading this blessing we should listen carefully to the beautiful parallelism that is expressed about God. Jacob recalls that his grandfather Abraham and his father Isaac walked before God, that God has been his shepherd all his life, and that the Angel has delivered him from all harm.

By Faith Jacob Blessed Joseph's Sons

God is "my Shepherd." It is a beautiful image, familiar to us from the well-known Psalm 23. The ancient shepherd was the one in authority over the flock of sheep, called upon to feed, to lead, and to defend the sheep in his care. Jacob confesses that this is what God has done for him throughout his entire life. Jacob was cared for in times of danger and want, but also in times of prosperity. By using the word "Angel" in parallel with God, Jacob is pointing out that God's very Angel, His own presence was by him all his life. But when does Genesis explicitly mention an Angel with Jacob? Genesis 32 recorded the night-long wrestling match, but it mentions first a "man" and then "God." Only Hosea 12:3–4 uses the word "Angel" to describe Jacob's wrestling opponent. Furthermore, Jacob says that this Angel delivered (or, redeemed) him from all harm.

Jacob's use of the word "Angel" in verse 16 is one of those places in the Old Testament that point out that the Lord Jesus Christ has been present throughout the story of redemption, directing people and events in such a way that God's elect have been protected—fed, led, and defended. God's people have God's Son with them even now (cf. Matt. 28:20), in the power of the Holy Spirit, so that we are kept in the love and care of our God all the days of our lives. Jacob could look back and confess that God had been a Good Shepherd to him. That same God is now going to bless Joseph's two sons so that they would be fruitful in this world.

Ephraim moved ahead of Manasseh (48:17–20)

Joseph initially is disturbed to see his father cross his arms so that the right hand blesses Ephraim, the younger, while the left hand blesses the older son, Manasseh. Joseph even tries to correct his father. But Israel knows exactly what he is doing. "I know, my son, I know." Hebrews 11 says that Jacob did this "by faith." Both tribes would be great, powerful tribes, but Ephraim would be the heart of northern Israel, "a group of nations," while Manasseh would be a "great people."

Israel assures Joseph of the future (48:21–22)

The two pillar promises in God's covenant promises in Genesis have been seed (descendants) and land.
The blessings pronounced have assured us of Joseph becoming two great tribes. But Joseph and his sons are still in the land of Egypt. Israel reassures Joseph that God will fulfill His own promise, made in Genesis 15 and often repeated: God will be with His children to bring them back to Canaan, the Promised Land. Even Joseph, who spends most of his life in Egypt, will have an inheritance in Canaan. Israel mentions a ridge of land (v. 22), although it is unclear what this refers to in the text earlier.
Perhaps the events of Genesis 34:25–29 are in the background here, but that is not agreed upon by all scholars.

Conclusion

Jacob has exercised his right as the great patriarch to alter the direction of his family's development. But he did this "by faith." We have witnessed a growth and maturity in his faith. By grace through faith Jacob embraced the promise of God for the future, and his blessing of double portion to Joseph is one way he can express it to Joseph, to Joseph's sons, and to us in the community of faith today.
Because every promise of God is "yes" and "amen" in Christ, we can live and also die by faith in His promises.

By Faith Jacob Blessed Joseph's Sons

Lesson 17: Points to ponder and discuss
1. Jacob tells his story briefly to Joseph and his sons. He draws attention to God's promises by faith. Why was it important to repeat this story (again!) to his son and grandsons? What is the reason that the Bible gives for us to repeat such testimony about God's deeds to our children? See Deuteronomy 6:4–9, 20ff. and Psalm 78:1–8.
2. In Genesis 48:11 Israel tells Joseph about the amazing turn of events that God has brought about in his life. Why did God put Israel through such things? What are similar things in your life where God has worked out some (great) changes, things that you never thought possible, humanly speaking?
3. God keeps us readers always a little off balance by doing unexpected things with unlikely people. God would do the very same thing in His Son, the Lord Jesus Christ. Show how this is true in the Person and work of Jesus Christ (e.g., where He was born, how He lived, what He possessed, etc.).
4. Read through Psalm 23 again. Trace Jacob's life in terms of what Psalm 23 describes (times of plenty, dangers, enemies, etc.). In other words, how did the LORD actually shepherd Jacob?

The Life of Jacob

5. The northern tribes were carried away, portion by portion, by the cruel Assyrians, until the fall of the city of Samaria in 722/721 B.C. Read Jeremiah 31:15–20. Over a century later the prophet Jeremiah would remind us of the LORD's heartfelt compassion for Ephraim. What did God want for Ephraim? What do we learn about our God in these statements about Ephraim?

6. "Seed and land": the pillar promises of the Old Testament covenants. But we are now in the new covenant era. How does that now apply to the promises God gives His church today?

Lesson 18

Jacob Tells His Sons About the Future

Read Genesis 47:29–31 and Gensis 49

Introduction: His "Last Will and Testament (49:1)
Jacob has spoken with Joseph and his sons about God's blessing upon them. Now he blesses all his sons. Genesis 49 contains the longest poetic portion of this book (vs. 2–27). This is often called "the blessing of Jacob" to his sons. Blessings in Scripture are also pregnant with the future. Jacob tells his sons to gather around so that he might tell them "what will happen" to them. The patriarch becomes a prophet, foreseeing the future by inspiration. But it is more that just the future. He also is judging his sons, that is, he evaluates their lives and speaks of where that will take matters in the future with respect to the tribes that will descend from them. As you read through Jacob's statements about his sons, it might be helpful to be looking at a map (in the back of most Bibles) of how the tribes were settled in Canaan.

My first three sons (49:2–7)
Leah bore four sons to Jacob initially: Reuben, Simeon, Levi, and Judah. Jacob speaks about them first, of course. Normally, the firstborn son was supposed to walk off with the double portion of blessing. That is what Reuben should have received, but he sinned against his father by becoming intimate with Bilhah, Rachel's maidservant (see Gen. 35:22). This was a sin against the 5th and 7th commandments. Such earlier sin now leads to this result. Sin had discredited

The Life of Jacob

him, and now he is disinherited as the firstborn. From later history, we never read of any king emerging from the tribe of Reuben. No prophet and no priest arise within the ranks of this tribe. On the contrary, in Numbers 16 we read about the revolt of Korah, Dathan, and Abiram—the last two men from the tribe of Reuben. They called into question the leadership of Moses, and the LORD punished them with death and destruction. "Turbulent as the waters, you will not excel," says Jacob about his firstborn son. And that is what happened. Reuben received his tribal land in the region east of the Dead Sea.

Jacob speaks of Simeon and Levi together. These two brothers banded together at the time of Dinah's violation by Shechem in Genesis 34. They hatched the plot that led to the massacre of the people of Shechem, something that had put Jacob in a very precarious position with the people of that region. Jacob recalls this about them, speaking about their "weapons of violence . . . they killed men in their anger." In fact Jacob curses their fierce anger and their cruel fury. Not much blessing here! His words are words of judgment. In the parallel lines in verse 7 Jacob says that these brothers (i.e., the tribes) will be "dispersed" in Israel.

And so it was . . . but in strangely different ways! It is a young man from Simeon (Num. 25:14) who boldly sins by bringing a Midianite young woman into his tent when God punished Israel during the Baal-Peor incident. Simeon is not even mentioned in Moses' blessing in Deuteronomy 33. Simeon receives land in the Promised Land, but it is in the dry southern portion of Canaan, and it is within the territory boundaries of the larger tribe of Judah. In other words, the dispersion of Simeon has them basically absorbed into another tribe.

Levi is also dispersed in Israel, but in a good way. It is the tribe of Levi that rallies to Moses' side at the sinful incident of the golden calf (see Exod. 32). Because of that loyalty to

Jacob Tells His Sons About the Future

the LORD and His cause, God "ordains" this tribe to be the priestly tribe that serves at the holy sanctuary of the LORD. Those Levites who do not serve at the sanctuary itself would be permitted to live throughout Israel in its towns and villages (see Num. 35:2, 7; Josh. 14:4; 21:41). It is a Levite, Phinehas, who takes a spear and boldly goes to impale the sinful Simeonite young man in the Baal-Peor incident mentioned above (see Num. 25:1ff.), and God blesses that zeal. So both Simeon and Levi are "dispersed" as Jacob says, but in strangely different ways.

Judah: a lion, a scepter, and a donkey (49:8–12)

Jacob's first three sons have "taken themselves out of the running," so to speak, by their sins of fornication and great violence. So now the patriarch sees into the future about Judah. Clearly he notes that this will be the royal tribe. Joseph may have authority over his brothers for the moment as they bow to him as ruler in Egypt. But the time will come when Judah's brothers will bow down to him. Jacob calls him a "lion's cub" (the lion as "king" of the beasts). He mentions a scepter and ruler's staff as staying with Judah "until he comes to whom it belongs" (pointing ahead to David and great David's greater Son, Jesus Christ). Rich imagery of a donkey tied to a vine fill out a picture of royalty and prosperity. Judah would occupy the southern hill country as a great and powerful tribe.

Zebulun and Issachar: in good land (49:13–15)

These two tribes occupied parts of the Galilee in the northern part of the Promised Land. Zebulun, technically not on the Mediterranean Sea, was close to the sea. Both tribes received land that was fertile. Plus, the men of Issachar became known for their spiritual insight, for they knew the times.

Dan: a serpent (49:16–18)

The name "Dan" comes from a word that speaks of justice or judging. "Dan will provide justice for his people," says Jacob. From Dan would come the great judge Samson (Judg. 13–16), but this tribe would also, in part, desert its tribal inheritance in order to migrate to northern Israel where it would cruelly attack a peaceful city and rename it . . . Dan! Danites would also engage in false worship, yielding to the wickedness of the great Serpent, Satan. "I look for Your deliverance, O LORD!" It is interesting to note that in the tribal roll call of Revelation 7:4–8, the tribe of Dan is not even mentioned.

Gad, Asher, and Naphtali (49:19–21)

Gad received his tribal land to the east of the Jordan River, sandwiched between Reuben to the south and half of Manasseh to the north. But this area would be vulnerable to attack by the Moabites from the south and by the Ammonites to the east.

Asher and Naphtali received their tribal land in the north, in the Galilee region as well as along the coast of the Mediterranean Sea. The land was fertile and rich, but that made it a desirable fruit to pluck on the part of foreign enemies. These tribes would not be able to drive out the Canaanites later on, and these tribes would be some of the first to be carried away by the Assyrians.

Joseph the vine and Benjamin the wolf (49:22–27)

Jacob comes to the "Rachel tribes" last. Certainly the longest comments are reserved for Joseph (sons Ephraim and Manasseh). Genesis 48 revealed that Jacob moved Joseph's two sons to the level of tribal patriarchs. These two tribes would become powerful and influential as Ephraim ("fruitful") would settle in the central hill country of the Promised Land, and Manasseh would live on both sides of

Jacob Tells His Sons About the Future

the Jordan River. Joshua would come from Ephraim, and this central tribe would be the last part of northern Israel that would go into exile to Assyria (722 B.C.).

At least two main points stand out in the blessing to Joseph. First, a complete picture of blessing is drawn in the words of Jacob. Do you hear these words: "fruitful vine . . . strong arms . . . blessings of the heavens . . . of the deep . . . of breast and womb"? Jacob had wondered in Genesis 37 concerning Joseph's dreams about the family having to bow down to Joseph. But now he acknowledges that the young son Joseph had become a "prince among his brothers" (v. 26). Second, Jacob gives God all the credit for this great blessing. It is all because of the "hand of the Mighty One . . . because of the Shepherd, the Rock of Israel . . ." In other words, "Praise God from whom all blessings flow!" So true for Joseph, but it remains absolutely true for all Christians today as well. "All things are yours," says the New Testament, and "you are Christ's, and Christ is God's."

The youngest son Benjamin (a "ravenous wolf") produced a tribe that became known for its excellent warriors. Ehud from Benjamin was a left-handed judge who killed the Moabite tyrant Eglon and led Israel to victory. Saul, Israel's first king, would come from Gibeah of Benjamin. But also during the time of the judges, civil war would nearly annihilate the tribe of Benjamin, a tragic story told in Judges 19–21. But from this tribe would later come another Saul in the book of Acts, a proud Pharisee who would be stopped by Jesus Christ and then transformed into the great Christian missionary of the New Testament, Paul.

Jacob gives instructions for his burial (49:29–32)

Jacob ends his days in the peace of knowing that Joseph was alive and that his large clan was living in peace and prosperity in the land of Goshen. Yet Jacob does not want his body to be buried in the Egyptian sand or in a royal pyramid or any other Egyptian final resting place. Egypt is not "home," no matter how "nice" it may be. In faith, he knows that the Promised Land is the place where "my people" are, he tells us (v. 29). He knows the address of his burial cave in Canaan. Abraham and Sarah, Isaac and Rebekah, as well as first wife Leah ("my people") are there. That, and nowhere else, is where Jacob insists on being buried. This is something that Jacob earlier had made Joseph solemnly swear, according to Genesis 47:29–31. Once this was promised, Jacob could worship "by faith . . . leaning on the top of his staff" (Heb. 11:21b). His heart was not in Egypt; he looked ahead to what God had promised him.

Jacob is "gathered to his people" (49:33)

The Bible tells us about Jacob's birth. He emerged from the womb with his small infant hand grasping his brother's heel. And now the Bible also tells us of his departure from this life: he "drew up his feet up into the bed, breathed his last and was gathered to his people." What a simple and beautiful description of the end of the life of this patriarch! The NIV Bible uses this as the heading above verse 29: "The Death of Jacob"—which is true—but the word "death" (both the verb and the noun) are not used in Genesis 49 to describe Jacob's departure. "Death" and "die" are used in chapters 48 and 50 but not here in this chapter. The last words from Jacob to his sons focus on his burial in the plot that had been purchased from the Hittites many years before.

When Jacob dies, Egypt mourns for him. But he is buried in the Promised Land, in the hope of his glorious resurrection. Still, in dying Jacob truly goes "to be with his people," for our God is the God of Abraham, Isaac, and Jacob. He is the God of the living, not of the dead. More than that, our Triune God is the God who elects His

Jacob Tells His Sons About the Future

own, before we have done anything good or evil in this world, and then He works steadily, for however long it may take, to wrestle us sinners down, to test and tame us, to put us "through many danger, toils, and snares," so that we might live by faith, and that we might die in His grace, always admitting that we are aliens and strangers in this earth (see Heb. 11:13–16).

May we see in the life of Jacob how God's amazing grace elects and then protects, guides and guards His own to the close of their lives. "Surely goodness and love will follow me all the days of my life, and I will dwell in the house of the LORD forever" (Ps. 23:6).

Lesson 18: Points to ponder and discuss

1. We do not know the day and hour when a loved one will leave this life. We do not dwell morbidly on this fact. Still, since this is the case that we do not know about their departure (should the Lord tarry), have you considered what *must* be said and done to those you know and love before that time comes? What do you *need* to say and do, especially with your loved ones, before the Lord calls you out of this life?
2. Jacob blesses these sons. Think back on the kinds of men they have shown themselves to be (the massacre at Shechem, selling their own brother Joseph, deceiving their father, etc.). Were they deserving of their father's blessing? How is Jacob both just and merciful in these final dealings with his sons? Does this parallel in some ways how the LORD God deals with us?
3. Read Luke 2:36–38. When Jesus was born, an old prophetess named Anna (Hannah), a descendant of the tribe of Asher, was present in the Temple. She went about speaking of the "redemption of Jerusalem" that had

The Life of Jacob

been born. As a tribe, Asher was taken away into captivity. Yet in Luke 2 there is a remnant present, saved by grace. How does this show the amazing grace of God, even centuries after the exile?

4. The tribe of Benjamin produced Saul, the first king, who persecuted David and tried to kill him. Later, another man of Benjamin, the Pharisee Saul, persecuted the Son of David, Jesus Christ. Read Acts 9:1–19, the conversion of Saul (later called Paul). How are those stories similar, and how are they different? Note how God rejected King Saul in the end, but He selected Paul to be His great apostle.

5. Jacob insists on having his body buried in Canaan, the Promised Land. Does it matter today where our bodies are to be buried? What and where is the "promised land" for us? What is the future for Christians, personally and corporately, in the age to come?

6. "To whom much is given, much is required."
When Jacob purchased the birthright from Esau, what covenantal responsibilities now became his? Could he have had any idea how God would lead his life from that point on? Could we have expected from Jacob the kind of speeches that he gives in Genesis 48 and 49, back in Genesis 25 and 27, earlier in his life? Grace elects and also sanctifies.

Notes

Notes

Notes

Notes

Notes